Freshwater Fisheries Management

Freshwater Fisheries Management

Severn–Trent Water Authority

Editor
Robin G. Templeton

Directorate of Technical Services

Area Fisheries Office

Fishing News Books Ltd

Farnham · Surrey · England

British Library Cataloguing in Publication Data
Freshwater fisheries management.
   1. Fisheries—Great Britain
   I. Templeton, Robin G   II. Severn–Trent
  Water Authority
   338.3′727092941   SH255
  ISBN 0-85238-130-1

Published by
Fishing News Books Ltd
1 Long Garden Walk, Farnham, Surrey, England

Photoset by Paston Press, Norwich
Printed in England by
Page Bros (Norwich) Ltd, Norwich

Contents

Appendices

List of figures

List of tables

Preface

This book has been written as a practical guide for anyone involved in freshwater fisheries management in the temperate regions. It is primarily concerned with fisheries management in the British Isles, but the principles set out here will have applications in many other countries and the legislation described will provide useful examples and guidelines to those involved in drafting statutory controls. Although each section is presented with the layman in mind, we hope that all serious students of freshwater biology will find the book a useful addition to the current literature.

The text is based on a series of pamphlets on fisheries management prepared by the authors for the Severn-Trent Water Authority, the Fisheries Department of which provides a service to any person requiring advice on fisheries management. For this book the contents of those pamphlets have been enlarged, and the range of topics extended by the addition of many new chapters. The accent throughout is on practical advice for the active fisheries manager. All the most common problems are covered here, and in those instances where space considerations preclude a full and detailed treatment it is hoped that the extensive bibliography and appendices will lead the reader quickly to further sources of more detailed or more specialized information.

Part 1 of the book describes the resource over which the fisheries manager holds responsibility. It subdivides naturally into a description of the physical environment inhabited by fish, followed by various aspects of fish biology and fish populations. With the scene thus set, Part 2 describes the principal techniques available to the manager for the management and improvement of that resource, be it by direct action such as the draining or desilting of a lake, or by indirect action such as the application of statutory or local regulations. Part 3 examines the commercial exploitation of the resource, with examples of the needs, methods and potential of angling, commercial fishing, and fish farming.

The eight appendices are aimed primarily at students of fisheries management in the United Kingdom and Eire, but again their

11

content will be found to have much wider application and relevance. Descriptions are given of the main organizations responsible for administration of fisheries, and of providing grants to fisheries developments. Information is given on careers in freshwater fisheries and on major employers in the field; and a summary is given of all current UK legislation relevant to fisheries management.

Acknowledgements

The main task of editing this book was undertaken by R G Templeton of the Severn-Trent Water Authority, with assistance from Dr B Broughton, Dr P E Bottomley and M L Parry. Individual chapters and parts of chapters were written by the following authors: B Broughton, M J Cathcart, A Churchward, M J Cooper, K W Easton, P Jarrams, R North, M L Parry, A Starkie and R G Templeton. In addition, many of the authors' colleagues in the Severn-Trent Water Authority made valuable contributions, and our appreciation extends to them all.

Most of the photographic material for the book was supplied and printed by M Ridgway. Additional photographs were supplied by Dr B Broughton, Mr K Easton and Mr M Hughes, all of STWA; Dr A Worthington; Prof. C Arme, University of Keele; Graham Wilson Photography, Mr P Thompson and V Holt.

The diagrams were prepared by the Drawing Office of STWA, with the exception of *Figures 74, 75, 76, 80* and *81* which appeared originally in *Salmon Fisheries of Scotland*, published by Fishing News Books in 1977 and were prepared by Mrs M Gammie, Illustrator at the Marine Laboratory, Aberdeen.

Finally our thanks are due to E Holmes and G E Fry for their care and patience in typing and retyping the various draft manuscripts.

While the individual authors must take much of the credit for their contributions, the production of this book would not have been possible without the full support of the Severn-Trent Water Authority.

The authors

All the contributors are or were employed with the Severn–Trent Water Authority during the period this book was produced. They have between them a wealth of experience in all aspects of fisheries management. They have written and had published many scientific papers: several of them write regular articles for the popular angling press.

The idea for the production originally came from **Robin Templeton.** He has been in the Water Industry since 1965 and has prior to his present appointment as Trent Area Fisheries Officer spent some time in Hampshire and Yorkshire. He graduated with a Zoology degree in 1961 and later gained an M Sc.

Michael Parry is the Regional Manager for Leisure Services and heads the Unit. Prior to joining the Severn–Trent in 1974 he spent several years with the Yorkshire River Authority after a period in Malaya as a Fisheries Officer. He graduated with a Biology degree in the late 1940s.

Peter Bottomley has been involved in fisheries and pollution work with the Severn–Trent Water Authority and its predecessors from 1952. He obtained his degree and doctorate and has a particular interest in water quality and fisheries.

Nigel Broughton (Bruno) has been with Severn–Trent Water Authority since 1978 and is now employed as a District Fisheries Officer in the Trent Area. He graduated with a Zoology degree and later obtained his doctorate.

Michael Cathcart was employed with the Severn–Trent Water Authority as a District Fisheries Officer, during the period 1971 to 1983. Prior to that he was with the fisheries section in Yorkshire after gaining several years experience in the legal profession.

Alan Churchward has been with the Severn–Trent Water Authority since 1972. Starting as a fisheries biologist he is now the Severn Area Fisheries Officer. After he graduated with a degree he obtained an M Sc in 1959. He has a particular interest in the commercial fisheries of the River Severn.

Martin Cooper graduated with a Biology degree in 1969. After several years working on trout farms in Scotland and Denmark he joined the Water Industry as a Pollution Officer in the Thames Area. He is now a Trent District Fisheries Officer.

Keith Easton has a biology degree and an M Phil. He has been with the Severn–Trent Water Authority since 1975 as a fish biologist in the Trent Area: his particular interest is in coarse fish culture.

Peter Jarrams has been in the Water Industry since 1966. He has reared various salmonids in Wales and at the Severn–Trent Water Authority fish farm near Nottingham and developed cage rearing facilities for the Severn–Trent Water Authority.

Rick North is a fish biologist, since 1975 with the Severn area. After graduating with a Zoology degree in 1971 he obtained his doctorate. His principle interest is in the biology of salmonids.

Alan Starkie has been with the Severn–Trent Water Authority since 1975 and is now a District Fisheries Officer. He graduated with a biology degree and later obtained his doctorate. His principle interest is in the biology of coarse fish.

Part 1: The resource

1.1 The aquatic environment

The aim of fishery managers was elegantly expressed by Richard Seymour in his book, *Fishery management and keepering* (1970) when he stated that, 'knowing and planning the fishery is . . . the first important step'. Whatever the ultimate reason for managing a fishery, the manager will find it easier if he has a basic understanding and appreciation of all aspects of the resource he is to manage, starting with the nature and use of water. It is then – and only then – that he can understand how fish have adapted to their environment and how best he can exploit and manage the whole resource.

Water

Water was crucial in the evolution of all living organisms, and biochemical systems are thus well adapted to function in aqueous solution. Moreover, aquatic life requires water as a support system and, in the case of animals such as fish, a medium in which to move and obtain a supply of oxygen. Terrestrial life also requires a regular supply of water to maintain its biochemical processes. Man uses water for drinking, cooking, laundry and bathing; for industrial processes and waste disposal; for cooling water for power-generating stations, and – in dry areas – for irrigation. The demand for water is great: in western Europe, for example, each person may use more than 200 litres of water per day for domestic purposes.

The water cycle

Water falling as rain or snow may travel along several different natural or man-directed paths (*Fig 1*). It will flow down a river or pass into groundwater, and may be stored in a reservoir, abstracted for domestic purposes, treated at a sewage works, or evaporate at any stage of the cycle. It can also be taken in by plants and used for conversion into carbohydrates by the process of photosynthesis, before being released again during the process of death and decay. It is essential to any fishery that there is a sufficient quantity of the right quality of water. A good fishery manager will appreciate that it is sometimes very difficult, if not impossible, to achieve this without a co-ordinated management plan covering an entire river catchment area – of which his fishery may be just a part.

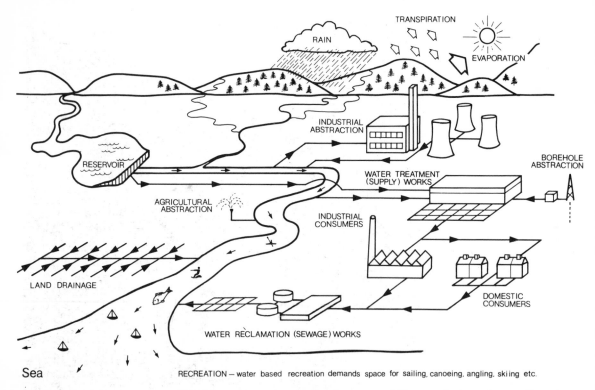

TRANSPIRATION

RAIN

EVAPORATION

INDUSTRIAL
ABSTRACTION

BOREHOLE
ABSTRACTION

RESERVOIR

WATER TREATMENT
(SUPPLY) WORKS

AGRICULTURAL
ABSTRACTION

INDUSTRIAL
CONSUMERS

LAND DRAINAGE

DOMESTIC
CONSUMERS

WATER RECLAMATION (SEWAGE) WORKS

Sea

RECREATION — water based recreation demands space for sailing, canoeing, angling, skiing etc.

Fig 1 The water cycle, showing how water falling as rain is used naturally or by
man before being recycled

Types of habitat   There is a vast range of freshwater habitats in which fish can live,
including mountain streams, slow-flowing lowland rivers, upland
tarns, small ponds and large reservoirs. Many books have been
written about the different types of freshwater habitat, but the basic
division is simply between flowing and stillwater.

From the fisheries aspect, flowing water can be sub-divided into
four zones, depending on the river-bed gradient and the water
velocity. These are described by the principal fish species present.
The trout zone (*Fig 2*) is characterized by the steepest gradient and
fastest current; this is then followed by the grayling and barbel zones,
and lastly the bream zone (*Fig 3*) which is very gentle in gradient and
slow flowing. In many rivers these zones may overlap or alternate.
Fish adapted to one zone may not necessarily survive in another
because they may not be able to tolerate the physical conditions. For
example, the maximum swimming speed of bream is only 0.6 metres
per second, whilst barbel can swim at up to 4.4 metres per second.
Bream are therefore unlikely to survive in the moderate-flowing
barbel reaches of a river where current velocity is in excess of 0.6
metres per second. It obviously makes little sense to stock fish into
conditions to which they are not or cannot become adapted.

Stillwaters provide a wide range and variety of living conditions for

16

Fig 2 A typical mountain stream characteristic of the trout zone in flowing waters, with inset trout

Fig 3 A lowland river characteristic of the bream zone of flowing waters, with inset bream

fish, and the most popular way of categorizing them is based on their biological features. Oligotrophic lakes are essentially nutrient-poor, and consequently never have obvious algal blooms or excessive plant growth; salmonids are the typical fish species present. Eutrophic lakes are nutrient-rich and support algal blooms and abundant plant growth; they may contain a wide variety of the coarse fish species. The term mesotrophic is sometimes used to describe those lakes intermediate in character between oligotrophic and eutrophic.

The total environment

Figure 4 shows how fish are related to the aquatic environment in which they live, and it can be seen that their relationships with other animals and plants form a cycle. In its most simple form, chemicals are taken up by plants which are eaten by invertebrates, and these in turn are eaten by fish. When fish die and decompose, their body chemicals are released and are available again for recycling. It is important to understand this cycle before any fisheries management operations are undertaken because they will, in some way or other, almost certainly alter the environment.

1.2 Water quality

It is a wise fisheries manager who discovers something of the quality of water in or flowing through his fisheries because even a brief study of water quality data can reveal factors that may have a significant or overriding effect on the number and type of fish that fishery can support.

Physical properties

Water has several physical properties that can directly or indirectly affect its quality (*Fig 5*).

Many of these physical properties, such as its surface tension,

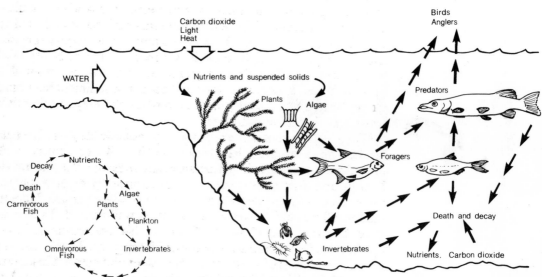

Fig 4 This diagram shows the relationship between fish, plants, animals and other factors in the aquatic environment – 'the aquatic food cycle'

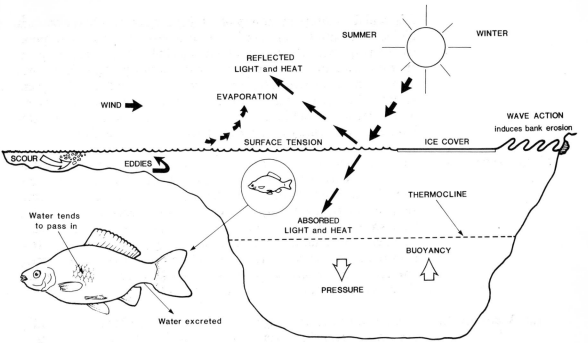

Fig 5 This diagram shows the range of physical properties of water

evaporation and viscosity, occur because of the way the two hydrogen atoms of the H$_2$O water molecule are bound to the oxygen atom. (There is an excellent explanation of this in the *Encyclopaedia Britannica*.) The net effect is that water is able to flow under the influence of gravity from a high altitude to one that is lower, and thence to the sea. One of the direct effects of this water movement is that during its passage it may scour or erode the land over which it flows. The amount of suspended solid material that is collected and carried *en route* will affect the water's suitability for supporting plant and animal life: at high levels it will increase the turbidity of the water, and therefore deprive plants of light that is essential for growth. When the current slows and the silt or sediment load can no longer be carried, it settles on the river-bed and may smother living organisms that inhabit this area.

Water is 700 times denser than air, and aquatic life therefore needs far less body support than land-based life. Water density is also influenced by changes in temperature and pressure. This means that in large and deep stillwaters during the warmer periods of the year, the warmer and less dense water rises to near the surface. Here it is influenced by surface winds and becomes well aerated. In contrast, water becomes most dense at 4°C, and at this temperature it sinks to the lake-bed and gradually becomes deoxygenated. In some large lakes, these zones of warm, less dense water and colder denser water are distinct, and separated from each other by an intermediate layer of water called a thermocline. In winter, when water tends to cool, that less than 4°C rises to the surface and a layer of ice may form. It often happens that twice a year the water becomes uniform in temperature and becomes mixed; if the lower layers are deoxygenated at these times, the subsequent 'overturn' can cause fish mortalities. The thermocline, where it is present, varies in depth from year to year and from water to water but it generally occurs at about 10m below the surface. In some of the newer and larger water supply reservoirs, mechanical means are provided to prevent this thermal stratification occurring: this is not for the benefit of fish but to prevent deoxygenated water from entering the water supply.

Water has the property of absorbing and storing radiant heat from the sun. Rapid overnight and seasonal temperature changes are therefore unusual, except in very shallow and exposed fisheries. Cold-blooded animals (poikilotherms) like fish therefore have a chance to adapt to slowly changing water temperature.

One additional and important property of water is that it will pass through a semi-permeable membrane from an area of low salt concentration into an area of high salt concentration by a process known as osmosis. Freshwater fish have body fluids that are more concentrated than the water in which they swim, and their skin acts as a semi-permeable membrane; they are therefore at risk of being waterlogged. They counteract this by possessing well-developed kidneys to excrete excess water and a protective layer of scales and mucus to help prevent too much water entering their bodies.

Chemical properties Water is a very good solvent for many different chemical compounds, and without these dissolved substances it would not be a suitable medium for aquatic life. All aquatic life requires certain minimum concentrations of various chemicals in order to exist. One of the main groups of soluble chemicals comprises the gases, and the two most important ones for aquatic life are oxygen and carbon dioxide. Each dissolves at a different rate in water, and the quantity dissolved is affected by temperature. At 5°C, for instance, water requires 12.7 milligrams per litre (mgl^{-1}) of oxygen to become saturated, whereas at 20°C this has decreased to 9.1 mgl^{-1}. When the quantity of oxygen exceeds saturation, water is said to be 'supersaturated'. This can happen in summer when abundant plant-life produces vast amounts of oxygen during sunny weather. It should be remembered that different fish have different minimum requirements of dissolved oxygen (DO) below which they will die (*Fig 6*).

Carbon dioxide is an essential raw material in the process by which plants make their food. This process is called photosynthesis, and is the means by which life on earth is kept going by capturing the sun's energy. Without this energy input life on this planet would run down and cease to exist. The sun's rays acting on chemicals in green plants enable them to convert carbon dioxide (dissolved in the water in the case of water-plants) and water into sugars and starches. These are

20

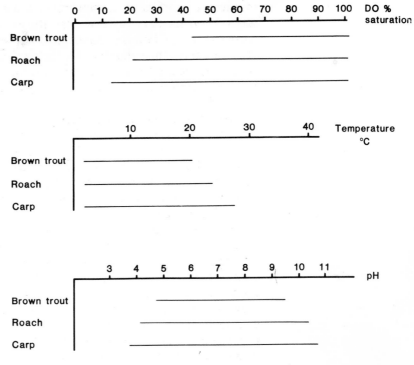

Fig 6 Approximate dissolved oxygen, temperature and pH range requirements for three species of fish

The minimum DO requirement depends on temperature, age, acclimation, carbon dioxide levels and pollutants present.
The upper lethal temperature depends on acclimation temperature eg brown trout acclimatised at 5°C - lethal temperature is 22.5°C acclimatised at 25°C - lethal temperature is 27.2.
Similar variation with roach and carp.

broken down inside the plant to provide the energy for growth and reproduction. During daylight carbon dioxide is removed from the water by green plants and oxygen is released. In darkness, oxygen is absorbed and carbon dioxide is released. Carbon dioxide is also a by-product of respiration, the process whereby plants or animals convert carbohydrates or sugars into energy, and an end-product of the oxidation processes of 'rotting' carried out by bacteria.

The demand for oxygen by bacteria is measured and expressed as the Biochemical Oxygen Demand (BOD). It is expressed as the amount of oxygen in a sample of water that is lost during a period of five days at 20°C, and is generally used to give an indication of the degree of organic pollution in water.

The water molecule in its normal state is split up into two types of electrically charged particles called ions – hydrogen ions (positively charged) and hydroxyl ions (negatively charged) – with both present in equal proportions. If another acid or alkaline base is added to the water, the balance of ions is altered. The degree of acidity or alkalinity is measured on a scale known as pH, which is simply a measure (on an inverse logarithmic scale) of the concentration of hydrogen ions in a given volume of water. A scale ranging from 1 to

14 is used. At a value of 7, water is said to be neutral; below 7 it is acid and above 7 it is alkaline. Most natural waters have a pH within the range 5.5 to 10 (with the majority being between 7.0 and 9.0). The existence of fish in waters outside this range is rare.

As rain falls through the air it absorbs carbon dioxide and levels may increase further as it percolates through the soil, especially in limestone or chalk areas. It thus becomes slightly acidic due to the carbonic acid formed, and readily dissolves the calcium present in the rock. The hardness of a water is principally a measure of the quantity of calcium bicarbonate $Ca(HCO_3)_2$ dissolved in the water, and levels can range from less than $20mgl^{-1}$ (soft) to over $300mgl^{-1}$ (very hard) expressed as $CaCO_3$. Hardness can affect the toxicity of certain metallic ions to fishes. For example, galvanized containers for fish are good when filled with hard spring water, but may cause fish to die if filled with soft moorland water. Aquatic plants need sufficient oxygen, carbon dioxide, a suitable range of water hardness and pH, nitrogen (as nitrate), phosphorus, silicon, potassium, magnesium, iron and other trace elements. In most hard waters these chemicals occur naturally; in eutrophic water there is an excess of certain essential chemicals (usually nitrates and phosphates) leading to an over-production of plant-life. The most common side effect of this is that plants produce excess oxygen as a by-product of photosynthesis in daylight, but at night they absorb oxygen from the water. When plants are very abundant they may cause night-time oxygen levels to fall so low that fish become asphyxiated. Under such conditions, plants also cause a night and day change in the pH level.

Waters with few dissolved substances are generally soft, and often drain peaty or insoluble rocky uplands. They support their own fauna and flora, but these are normally impoverished compared with those of nutrient-rich areas.

A measure of the total quantity of dissolved chemicals in a water sample can be obtained by measuring its electrical conductivity expressed as micro-siemens per cubic centimetre ($\mu S/cm^3$), and high figures indicate high concentrations of chemicals. On rivers that receive saline waste water from coal mines, for instance, conductivities may be in excess of $2\,000\mu S/cm^3$; the mountain streams that flow across granite may have conductivities below $100\mu S/cm^3$.

A good example of the way in which nutrients are cycled is provided by the nitrogen cycle which begins with the uptake of nitrate for the manufacture of protein. When the plant or animal dies, and fully decomposes, ammonium ions (NH_{4+}) are released and these then become oxidized again to <u>nitrite</u> and eventually to <u>nitrate</u>. A chemical analysis of the amount of ammonia present gives an indication (with BOD) of the degree of organic pollution in a water.

The amount of chloride in a water (its salinity) is also a useful measure in a water sample. Chloride can range from less than $10mgl^{-1}$ to over $25\,000mgl^{-1}$ (in seawater). Chloride levels increase slightly below sewage discharges, although the levels produced as a result have no harmful effects on freshwater organisms.

Interpretation of water quality data One of the questions that is most frequently asked of water quality data is 'will this water support more fish?' In order to answer this, and to interpret water quality analysis data, the results are often compared with those of other fisheries.

For convenience it is usual to express the results of a chemical analysis of water quality in the form shown in *Table 1*. The pH is measured on its own scale; most other chemicals are measured by weight, in milligrams per litre. The actual quantities of the various chemicals are thus extremely small. Some substances, such as nitrate (which is always combined with a metal, or with ammonium) are measured by reference to the nitrogen (N) they contain. BOD, the measure of organic activity in the water, is measured by the amount of oxygen the water sample absorbs as a result of this activity under standard laboratory conditions.

Typical water analyses, all from waters suitable for fish to live in, are shown below. The table illustrates the range of chemicals, and measurements expected, from a typical limestone borehole or chalk stream, a large Midland river, and a South Pennine reservoir. (The figures show the extremes where more than one river is sampled, or where more than one sample is taken from the same river.) The chalk

Table 1 EXAMPLES OF WATER QUALITY DATA FROM THREE DIFFERENT LOCATIONS

	Limestone/ chalk stream	*Midland river*	*Pennine reservoir*
pH	7.9–8.7	7.2–7.9	6.0–6.9
Temperature °C	8.0–15.0	4.0–24.0	4–18
Dissolved oxygen (mgl^{-1})	10–12.6	7.6–12.2	Saturated
Conductivity (micro-siemens)	380–500	640–1090	99–119
BOD $(mgl^{-1}$ as $O_2)$	0.7–4.2	2.0–6.7	1.0–2.8
Chlorides $(mgl^{-1}$ as Cl)	35–42	50–130	9–14
Nitrates $(mgl^{-1}$ as N)	8.5–9.8	5.2–10.3	0.5–1.2
Ammonia $(mgl^{-1}$ as N)	0.1–0.5	0.1–0.8	0.001–0.06
Hardness $(mgl^{-1}$ as calcium carbonate)	165–210	233–445	32–41
Suspended solids (mgl^{-1})	0–5.0	7–94	2–8

stream and the Midland river tend to have greater quantities of chemicals present in them than the Pennine reservoir. Consequently both produce a greater quantity of plant material and/or plankton for invertebrates, and thus potentially more food for fish. The Midland river carries a larger volume of treated effluent than the limestone water and this is reflected in higher levels of conductivity, ammonia and nitrates. Natural waters that are enriched with effluent in this way tend to provide ideal conditions for coarse fisheries. Conversely, extreme levels of some chemicals, and high temperatures, will restrict the all-year round suitability of such waters for salmon and trout.

It must be remembered that there are seasonal and daily changes in the quantity of chemicals present in any water. In the ideal world it would be useful to have samples taken continuously, but this obviously is not normally possible. Samples are therefore taken at the times of year when conditions are likely to be at their most extreme, *ie* in summer or winter. When only one sample is available, or when samples taken at different times of year are being compared, other evidence (such as the presence or absence of certain invertebrate animal species) should be considered before assessing a water as a fishery. Separate species of fish have their own levels of tolerance to different concentrations of chemicals and also to different temperatures. *Figure 6* shows the ranges of temperature, pH and DO suitable for trout, roach and carp.

When interpreting water quality data, it is important to remember that an alteration or change in the level of one chemical, or a change in one physical feature, will affect another. An increase in temperature, for example, will usually decrease the level of DO.

Main types of pollution   Most of us think of pollution as being something caused solely by the activities of mankind, but there are many examples of natural pollution – waters with a low pH because of run-off from peaty boglands; waters at the bottom of deep lakes that become deoxygenated; and so on. These, however, fall outside the definition of pollution used here, which is that used by D Mills in his book *Salmon and Trout* in 1971. He considers that,

> 'the natural state of pure water is sometimes upset by man when he allows poisonous substances to enter rivers in order to be diluted and carried away. These substances are in liquid form, and when discharged into the river are known as effluents. Effluents are the waste products of industrial processes or domestic activities and contaminate the water. Such contamination is known as pollution'.

There are three main categories of pollution, each based on the effect that it has on the environment, the fish and other aquatic life (*Fig 7*).

The first category covers poisons, including acids and alkalis: the list is long, but includes chromium salts from tanning and electroplating; phenols and cyanides from chemical industries and coal carbonization; copper, lead and zinc from various industries and mines; insecticides from agriculture, forestry, sheep dips and carpet manufacture. It is worth noting that some of these substances are rapidly precipitated in the receiving water (*eg* copper and lead when they run into hard water), but others are more persistent. These poisons usually enter the fish through its gills, and will kill it if present in a

24

Fig 7 Fish killed by water
pollution

sufficiently high concentration. Fish may try, but will not always succeed, in swimming away from poisons.

The second category of pollution includes all suspended solids, the light or finely divided suspended matter which does not settle quickly but makes the water opaque or cloudy. Washing processes associated with mining or quarrying can cause this, as can the washing of root crops. Its immediate effect is to prevent light penetrating the water, thus affecting plant growth. Ultimately such suspended particles settle out and can literally smother and kill all plant and invertebrate life; and if continuously present in large amounts can prevent their growth. This effect can also render gravel unsuitable for trout and salmon spawning by clogging up the spaces between the stones. Where excessive concentrations of suspended solids occur, fishes' gills may be irritated, thus affecting their respiratory process. Protective mucus may also be removed, making it easier for infections of bacteria, fungi and other diseases to enter the body. In extreme cases gill lamellae become blocked and fail to function.

25

The third category of pollution includes organic residues. Deoxygenation of the water is often caused when these organic materials decompose by the action of bacteria, and the degree of this organic pollution is usually assessed by the BOD test already described. Fortunately, rivers are to some extent self-purifying, with the harmful effects of organic pollution usually being oxidized out of the system downstream from the point of entry. The degree and speed of this self-purification is dependent on the quantity of the organic effluent, the size of the river, and how much aeration it receives as it flows downstream. The number of weirs and riffles, for instance, can increase the rate of oxygen uptake in the water and so speed purification. The list of sources of organic waste includes dairies, silage plants, manure heaps, sugar beet factories, textile factories, canneries, breweries, fish meal factories and domestic sewage works. The effect on the river below any point of discharge, particularly if the river is too small to dilute the effluent, is to stimulate the growth of bacteria in the river. These growths in turn lower the oxygen level in the water. This can kill fish by suffocation if the oxygen levels fall too low, or if the fish do not move away from the polluted area.

These then are the three main categories of pollution, but there are others. High water temperatures can make stretches of river unsuitable for certain species (or in extreme cases, all species) and may occur as a result of the waste warm water released by some power stations. Oil is usually visually more dramatic than most other types of pollution: a gallon (4.54l) of oil, for example, can spread out over about 2ha of water surface! There is also a real danger of the water becoming deoxygenated if the oil coverage persists for any amount of time, as contact is lost between water and air. It can also taint the flesh of fish, so this must be borne in mind if the fish caught are going to be eaten.

Responsible authorities   The Water Authorities in England and Wales (*Fig 8*) have the major responsibility of supplying clean water to, and disposing of waste water (sewage) from, the consumers in their area of operation, a responsibility that was clearly defined in the 1973 Water Act. Furthermore, each Water Authority has a duty to provide such sewers as may be necessary to drain its area and to treat the contents of such sewers. The basic objective of water reclamation (sewage treatment *etc*) is to produce a treated effluent that may be discharged without affecting other water users. Consequently, Water Authorities impose control over all discharges in their areas, including those from their own water reclamation works. These controls include discharges to underground aquifers and the discharge of industrial effluents, be they to a sewage works or directly into a river.

As a matter of routine all Water Authorities take regular samples of water throughout their area. This continual monitoring helps

26

Fig 8 Water Authority areas
in England and Wales

them to ensure that in the first place the quality condition attached to consents to discharge can be controlled, and secondly that these are having the desired effect on the receiving river. It is vitally important, however, to realize that no matter what legal powers there are to control pollution, there is always the risk of accidental discharges. If this happens it may be vital for the first person to notice the pollution (often an angler) to report the incident immediately to the appropriate Authority.

1.3 Water quantity   The water cycle described in the introduction showed how water falling as rain could follow several different paths. The field of science concerned with the natural component of the water cycle is known as hydrology.

27

Measurement techniques   To aid water management, hydrologists measure catchment rainfall, water losses (to evaporation and to the underground strata) and river flow. River flows in all Water Authority areas are continuously monitored by purpose-built gauging stations (*Fig 9*). In the Severn-Trent Water Authority area (*see Fig 8*) there are 100 such installations. All major rivers have at least one continuous record of the quantity of flow, and occasional spot flow measurements are also made on an informal basis. Details of all such data are published regularly. Any fisheries manager can obtain an approximate estimate of the speed of river flow if he follows the sequence described in *Figure 10*.

Water abstractions   The Water Resources Act 1963 changed some of the common law rights of riparian owners. In 1965/66 owners who had for the five previous years been abstracting water were allowed a set period in which to apply, under that Act, for a 'Licence of Right'. Each Water Authority is under a duty to conserve, redistribute or augment water resources for their area.

Fig 9 A purpose-built gauging station in the area of the Severn-Trent Water Authority

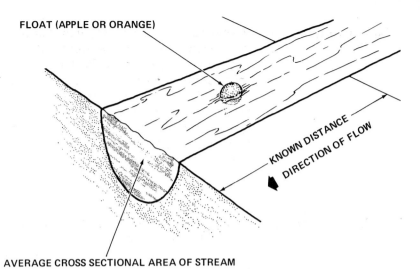

FLOAT (APPLE OR ORANGE)

KNOWN DISTANCE

DIRECTION OF FLOW

Fig 10 A simple and quick way to obtain an approximate measure of stream flow

AVERAGE CROSS SECTIONAL AREA OF STREAM

A VERY ROUGH ESTIMATE OF FLOW CAN BE MADE BY MEASURING THE AVERAGE WIDTH AND DEPTH OF WATER (WHERE THE CHANNEL IS REASONABLY UNIFORM) AND NOTING THE TIME IN SECONDS TAKEN BY AN APPLE , ORANGE, OR PIECE OF WOOD TO FLOAT OVER A KNOWN DISTANCE UNDER CONDITIONS OF STILL AIR. THE AVERAGE SPEED OF FLOW OF WATER IN A CHANNEL IS ABOUT 0.8 OF THE SURFACE VELOCITY IN MID-STREAM SO THAT THE SPEED OF FLOW SHOWN BY THE FLOAT SHOULD BE CORRECTED BY MULTIPLYING IT BY 0.8.

THE VOLUME OF FLOWING WATER IS OBTAINED BY MULTIPLYING THE CROSS-SECTIONAL AREA IN SQUARE FEET BY THE (CORRECTED) SPEED OF FLOW IN FEET PER SECOND, WHICH WILL GIVE THE ANSWER IN CUBIC FEET PER SECOND. THIS FIGURE MAY BE CONVERTED TO GALLONS PER SECOND BY MULTIPLYING BY 6¼; TO GALLONS PER MINUTE OR PER HOUR BY MULTIPLYING BY 60 OR 3600.

ALTHOUGH THIS IS A QUICK METHOD, THE RESULTS CAN ONLY BE VERY APPROXIMATE BECAUSE OF THE ERRORS IN TIMING. IT IS IMPORTANT TO TAKE A SERIES OF READINGS AND TO AVERAGE THESE.

Rivers of good quality with an adequate flow of water are essential for fisheries and other recreational pursuits. Most industries needing water, for example agriculture's need for irrigation water and the needs of power stations for cooling water, require a licence to abstract water. The would-be abstractor has to make written application to the Authority for a licence, and place an advertisement of his intention in the *London Gazette* and in a local newspaper. Objectors to the proposal then have twenty-eight days in which to make written representation to the Water Authority. If the applicant is dissatisfied with the Authority's decision he may appeal to the Secretary of State for the Environment. Angling clubs and fishery owners need therefore to check their local newspapers for applications, or join one of the national angling organizations who monitor all applications in the *London Gazette*. It is worth knowing that the Water Abstraction Licensing Section in a Water Authority will usually consult the Fisheries Section before granting a licence.

There are a number of exemptions under the Water Resources Act in that the fishery owner may have a 'protected right'. The effect of this is that the Water Authority is precluded from granting a licence that would derogate from a protected right. If a Water Authority, in breach of its duty not to do so, grants a licence that derogates from the protected right, then the owner who is entitled to that protected right may take court action for damages against the authority.

Licences to abstract may contain clauses referring to a 'prescribed minimum flow', below which the abstraction should cease. Angling organizations considering purchasing or leasing waters (see Section 3.2) are well advised to check with their local Water Authority to ensure their proposed fishery is not subject to problems with low flow. Conflict may occur, for example, when a farmer requires water for growing crops or for providing water for cattle – thereby reducing the amount of water to below that necessary for successful fishing.

1.4 Basic fish biology

The freshwater fish of the British Isles are of four principal types:

- Fish of the family Salmonidae, *eg* salmon, brown trout and rainbow trout. These are both migratory and non-migratory, and are generally cold water fish adapted to fast-flowing water.
- Non-predatory coarse fish, most of which belong to the family Cyprinidae. This family is characterized by the carp and contains the largest number of species in the British Isles. Its members are all freshwater species and the habitats they colonize vary from upland streams, with clean water and inhabited by barbel, to lowland marshy areas inhabited by bream and tench. In the intermediate habitats live chub, dace, roach and others.
- Predatory coarse fish, of which pike and perch are the most widespread species. This group has been enlarged by the introduction and spread of the zander.
- Non-angled species, an arbitrary grouping composed of small species such as minnow, stone loach, bullhead and stickleback.

There are around 50 species of freshwater fish in Britain and all can be identified with the aid of a suitable key, (*see reading list*).

To understand fish biology, a knowledge of the structure of fish is needed. Most European freshwater fish are variations on a similar basic pattern.

As fish are poikilotherms (cold-blooded animals) their body temperature fluctuates in the same way as the temperature of the water surrounding them. Basic metabolism rates will increase with increasing temperature and decrease with decreasing temperature. Thus any change in temperature will have a consequent effect on the rate of any chemical reactions taking place in the fish. This temperature dependence is perhaps the single most important factor influencing fish biology and thus behaviour.

Movement

The external features of a fish are shown in *Figures 11* and *12.*

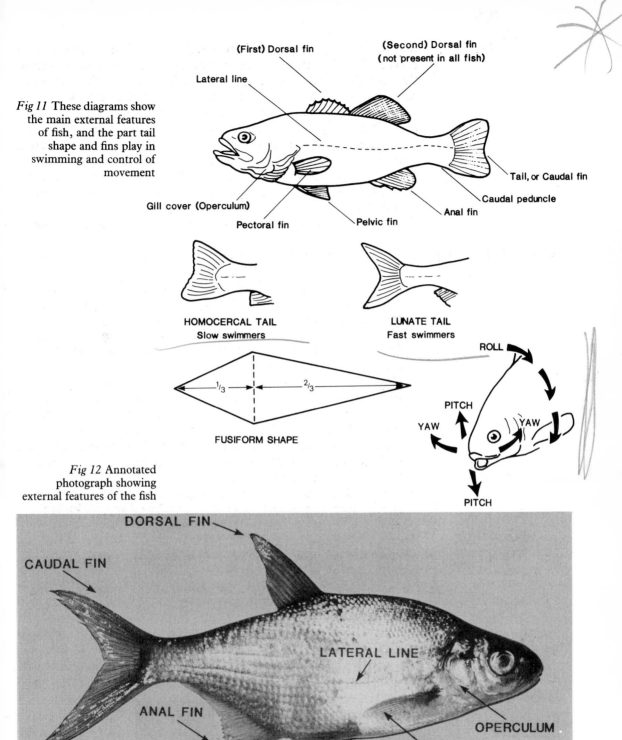

Fig 11 These diagrams show the main external features of fish, and the part tail shape and fins play in swimming and control of movement

(First) Dorsal fin

(Second) Dorsal fin (not present in all fish)

Lateral line

Tail, or Caudal fin

Caudal peduncle

Anal fin

Gill cover (Operculum)

Pectoral fin

Pelvic fin

HOMOCERCAL TAIL
Slow swimmers

LUNATE TAIL
Fast swimmers

1/3   2/3

FUSIFORM SHAPE

ROLL

PITCH

YAW   YAW

PITCH

Fig 12 Annotated photograph showing external features of the fish

DORSAL FIN

CAUDAL FIN

LATERAL LINE

ANAL FIN

OPERCULUM

PECTORAL FIN

PELVIC FIN

31

Propulsion of the fish is achieved by sideways movements of the body that cause the tail fin to move from side to side. The fin rays bond as they press against the water and the angle they take forces the fish forward. Different species have tails shaped to suit their speed of swimming: the more the tail approaches the shape of a crescent moon, the faster the fish can swim (*see Fig 11*). Fins are used for keeping the fish moving straight, and for manoeuvering, and they control the fish in the three planes of pitch, roll and yaw.

Fish species possess different shapes which enable them to adapt to their own particular environment. The faster fish (*Fig 13*) are streamlined or fusiform in their shape, and the maximum width and depth of their bodies is about one third of the way along from head to tail. There are many variations on this shape depending upon the environment in which the fish lives. Rudd, for instance, have a shape which is totally different from that of eels.

Skin and colouration

Another feature of the skin is its colour, and this is almost always related to the need for camouflage. Predatory fish like pike and zander have bars of different colour on their flanks to break up their outline and make them more difficult to see by their prey. Surface-living fish such as bleak and dace have silver bellies as this makes them blend into the surface when viewed from below. Bottom-dwelling fish like carp (*Fig 14*) and tench are dark green or brown, the colour of the weeds and the bottom of the lake or stream.

The skin also provides the first defensive barrier against disease and parasites, and a fish is more susceptible to infection if this barrier is broken (*Fig 15*). It is important to bear this in mind when moving fish in and out of their environment for fisheries management

Fig 13 Streamlined, fusiform, shape of a leaping salmon

32

Fig 14 Carp feeding – note the dark body colouring typical of a bottom dwelling fish

Fig 15 Roach showing damage to scales, through which disease may enter

purposes. In very cold conditions, when a fish's metabolism is slow, damage inflicted may not be repaired in time to prevent infection becoming serious.

Senses   Other external features of a fish include the eyes, the mouth, the nostrils and the lateral line, and these are all connected to the internal organs of the fish (*Fig 16*).

Fig 16 The main internal organs and muscles of a fish are shown in this diagram

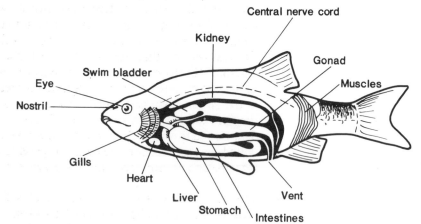

The eyes of a fish are paired and are located at either side of the front of the head to give them a good field of vision. Fish like pike (*Fig 17*) have good binocular vision (*ie* depth vision) because their eyes are well forward; tench (*Fig 18*) have eyes set more on the side of their heads where they are sensitive to movement but where the binocular vision is poorly developed. The eyes of some fish are bigger and better developed than others – carp, for example, have well developed eyes whereas those of eels and lampreys are small.

The nostrils of fish are paired and normally in front of and just below the eyes. These allow a current of water to enter a sense organ

Fig 17 The location of eyes well forward on the head allow good binocular vision as in this pike

Fig 18 The location of eyes on the side of the head, as in this tench, allow sensitivity to movement but poorly developed binocular vision

just behind the nostrils. This sense organ is a sac lined with thousands of small cells each of which detect smell. The ability to detect chemicals in solution varies from species to species, although many fish have an acute sense of smell: eels, for example, can detect certain substances at concentrations equivalent to a few drops in the whole of the North Sea.

The lateral line of a fish comprises a band of cells, sensitive to low-pitched vibrations, that normally shows up as a line along the flanks. By using this lateral line, fish are very aware of noise in the environment and can detect vibrations quite a long distance away. For this reason, this lateral line sense is sometimes called 'touch at a distance'. Outboard motors, for instance, produce a large amount of underwater noise which travels much better underwater than it does in the air, and fish have been shown to avoid such sounds even when they are distant. Fish have internal ears but as sound carries a great deal better in water than in air, they have no eardrums or earflaps. Allied to the ears are balancing organs that provide the fish with information on how upright or otherwise it is.

Digestion The most obvious external feature of a fish is the mouth, which enables the animal both to breathe and eat. To eat, fish take up food into the mouth, taste it, and swallow it by a suction type of action. All fish in the carp family have throat or pharyngeal teeth which grind the food upwards onto a hard pad so as to crush it before it enters the gut. The design of these teeth is specific to each species and their inspection is one of the only means of distinguishing them. The rest of the gut is concerned with the secretion of digestive juices (enzymes) and the absorption of food. The undigested remains of this food are passed out as faeces from the vent at the rear of the fish.

Respiration To breathe, fish take water into the mouth with the gill cover (operculum) closed, then close the mouth, open the gill cover, and raise the floor of the mouth. This pumps the water through the gills. Oxygen passes from the water into the blood through the semi-permeable membrane of the gill. The blood flow is in the opposite direction to that of the water (called the counter-current principle) so as to obtain the best oxygen uptake. If water flowed in the other direction (*ie* into the gill cover and out through the mouth), the fish could not extract enough oxygen from the water and could drown.

Fish gills are both sensitive and delicate. Air contains 20% oxygen by volume, but water contains only 0·001% at 8°C. Gills are therefore very efficient at extracting oxygen from water, given that there is a sufficient flow of water over them.

Nervous system The brain is in the middle of the head. It communicates directly to a spinal cord which sends and receives messages to and from the muscles and the rest of the body. The brain of a fish is relatively long,

35

with well developed areas relating to the senses that are important to the fish. The olfactory lobes are often very large as many fish depend on a good sense of smell. The 'higher' brain centres found in mammals are not present in fish so it may be speculated that they live at a lower level of consciousness than warm-blooded vertebrates, and lack rational thought processes.

Reproduction
The reproductive organs of fish are internal. Females carry paired ovaries which rapidly increase in size as the spawning season approaches: just prior to spawning, they may comprise one-fifth of the total body weight. Males have paired testes which do not reach the size ovaries attain. Both the eggs and milt are shed from an opening near the vent into the water, or onto gravel or plants, when the fish are spawning. Fertilization is therefore external. With the exception of tench where the male and the female have differently shaped pelvic fins, it is difficult to distinguish male from female fish using external features alone. In some species size is a good guide (a pike over 5kg is almost certainly female), whereas in others (*eg* carp) size and sex are not linked.

1.5 Food and food-chains
The processes that comprise the external and internal biology of fishes are often referred to collectively as the 'whole animal response'. It is this that fisheries management attempts to influence, either directly or indirectly. Ecology and the balance of nature in the context of fisheries management are the subject of this section.

What is ecology?
Ecology is the study of the way in which plants and animals relate to their environment. One of the first ecological principles is that plants and animals are a product of their own particular environment and did not, do not, and can never exist apart from that environment. Some of these environmental factors have been described in earlier sections of this book and should be regarded as being indivisible from the welfare of fish.

Food-chains
The relationship between an animal's food and what predates on it is termed a food-chain or food cycle (*Fig 19*). There are different levels of food producers within this chain, with a limited number of consumers at each so called trophic level. Normally, there is a reduction of biomass (*ie* that mass of animals or plants associated with any particular level) of around 10 to 1 from any one level to the next higher level. This occurs when, say, freshwater shrimps eat plants, or roach eat freshwater shrimps. The best way to understand this food-chain is to consider it as a pyramid of numbers (*Fig 20*). Thus, any one factor affecting one level will indirectly affect levels further up or down the chain. It follows that predators must, by definition, be far less numerous than the fish on which they feed.

Consider a lake with a healthy fish population of roach and pike.

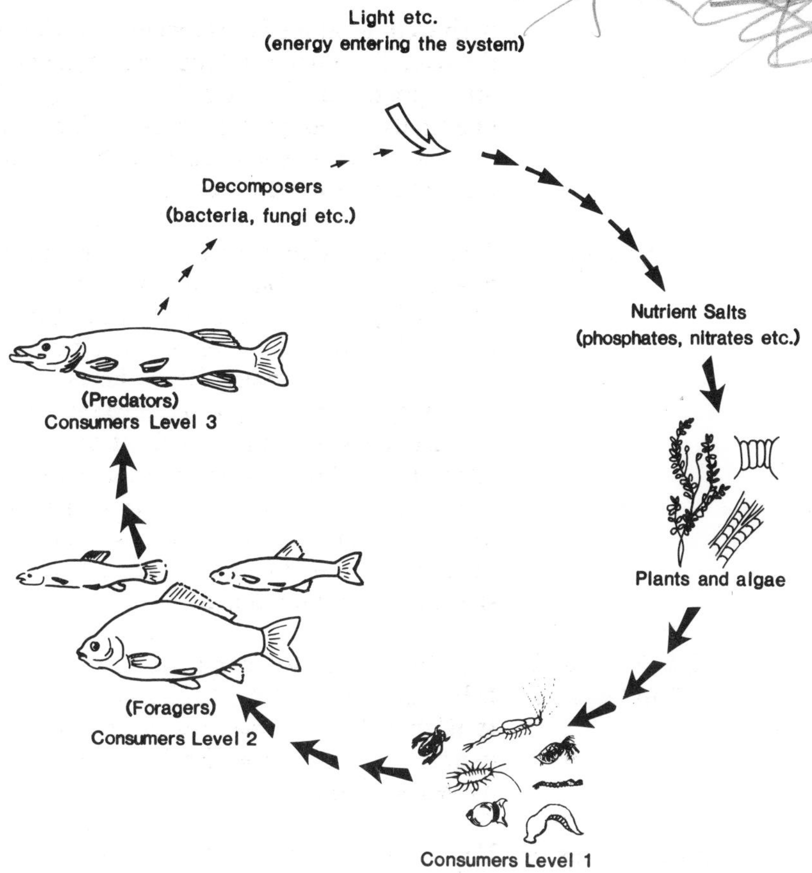

Light etc.
(energy entering the system)

Decomposers
(bacteria, fungi etc.)

Nutrient Salts
(phosphates, nitrates etc.)

(Predators)
Consumers Level 3

Fig 19 The relationship between different aquatic animals and plants is shown in this 'freshwater food cycle'

Plants and algae

(Foragers)
Consumers Level 2

Consumers Level 1

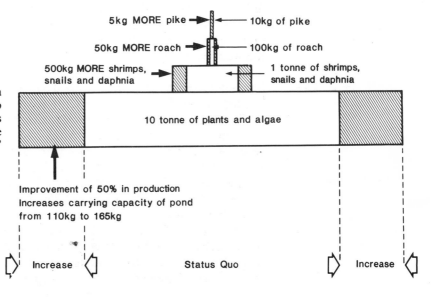

5kg MORE pike → | ← 10kg of pike

50kg MORE roach → | ← 100kg of roach

500kg MORE shrimps, snails and daphnia → | ← 1 tonne of shrimps, snails and daphnia

Fig 20 There is a quantitative relationship between plants and animals in a pond known as the 'pyramid of numbers'

10 tonne of plants and algae

Improvement of 50% in production
Increases carrying capacity of pond
from 110kg to 165kg

Increase   Status Quo   Increase

The plants and algae which grow there are eaten at all stages by such aquatic invertebrates as snails, freshwater shrimp and water hoglouse. These in their turn are eaten by the roach. Pike chase and catch the roach, eat and digest them, and grow accordingly. The aim of most pike anglers is to catch a 10kg fish – and that of the fishery manager is to provide such a fish. This 10kg pike must have eaten ten times its own weight in roach (100kg), which together will have eaten 1 000kg of snails, shrimps *etc*. They in turn, will have eaten 10t of weed and algae. The energy to form this weed comes from the sun. This whole system is in a state of dynamic balance which is often called the balance of nature, but this term is misleading as it implies a degree of stability that may or may not be present in the system.

There may be little or no actual loss of nutrients in a lake that has neither a feeder stream not an outflow, because the original materials are recycled many times over. Waste matter excreted by fish and other animals, for example, provides a valuable nutrient source for the plants, and the carbon dioxide given off during respiration contributes to the carbon source. Any organism that dies is broken down by the action of decomposers – the aquatic bacteria which play an important role within the food-chain. (This breaking down process also occurs when animals such as water hog-lice and caddis larvae eat detritus and excrete waste products). It is as important to provide good conditions for decomposers as it is for producers. For instance, the bacteria responsible for making ammonia non-toxic to fish by converting it to nitrate are aerobic, that is, they need oxygen. If the lake or pond bottom is anaerobic and lacks oxygen, very few of these bacteria will survive and this cuts down the recycling of nitrogen in the lake, which in turn may limit plant growth.

As well as the nutrients that are taken into the bodies of animals and plants, light energy is put into the system. This is used to fix atmospheric carbon dioxide and there is also an inflow of nutrients from other outside sources. The source of material may be of great importance in small streams where up to 80% of the nutrients may be obtained from the breakdown of introduced organic matter such as leaves and grass. Thus, the whole balance can be seen to be one of a dynamic flow of energy through different levels in the food-chain.

The factors therefore that govern the number of animals at any level are:

- The number of predators.
- The number of prey (*ie* the number of animals at the level below).
- The number of individuals at each level (*ie* the competition between individuals of the same or different species).

If animals or plants at any particular level are not being eaten they may simply become overcrowded and compete so much for the available food or space that they become stunted. A similar effect may become apparent when predators are removed. Their absence may allow the numbers of animals in the level below to grow unchecked. This is often the consequence of the killing and removal of pike from a small fishery which then becomes over-populated with stunted prey fish.

The role of the habitat   Any one of the levels may get out of control in a lake or pool when, say, the drainage entering it brings with it some of the nitrates used to fertilize the surrounding land. The balance of the levels may have to be restored by removing a certain number of individuals at a particular level, and this concept of 'culling' or 'cropping' is a necessary tool for the management of certain fisheries for specific angler use. This might entail removing weed, culling predators, or reducing the numbers of roach or other coarse fish.

The carrying capacity of a water is of great interest to fisheries managers because the whole of the food-chain is related to water chemistry, sunlight, and nutrients entering the system. There is a well-defined ceiling at which each of the levels in the food-chain can operate, and this effectively limits the number of fish that can be supported there. The sizes and number of fish can vary within certain limits, but it is normally the case that there is a maximum living weight (biomass) of fish that a water can support. If, for instance, a fishery can hold 500kg of roach, this can comprise $1\,000 \times 0\cdot5$kg fish or $2\,000 \times 0\cdot25$kg fish. Manipulation of fish stocks within the carrying capacity is a subject dealt with in the next section. It is possible, though, to improve the habitat so as to increase its overall ability to support aquatic life.

The importance of fish food   It is obvious that to increase the number of fish in a fishery, the whole pyramid of numbers has to be broadened (*see hatched sections on Fig 20*). It is futile merely to stock it with more fish without increasing the amount of food, because this will merely unbalance the pyramid. The most effective way of increasing the carrying capacity is to broaden the base of the pyramid by increasing the primary production of plants and algae so that this can have a 'knock on effect' upwards. For average lakes in the Midlands of England, a figure of 350kg of fish per hectare is often the effective maximum biomass of fish that can be supported. In streams, the variation can be much greater.

1.6 Monitoring and controlling fish stocks   One of the key questions asked in relation to river or lake management is 'How many fish does our water contain?' This is often followed by the questions, 'How many should it hold?', and, 'If the right management techniques are applied, how many could it hold?' It is therefore extremely important to gain a good knowledge of the stock of fish present in a fishery. Once this is known, the techniques required to increase or decrease this stock can be applied. This

39

chapter describes some of the techniques used to capture fish, estimate numbers in a fish population, control stock numbers, and keep records.

Fish capture techniques   There are many techniques available for fish capture, but for practical purposes they can be grouped in four sections.

Seine netting

The most easily applied technique for capturing fish is the use of a seine net. This is a simple wall of netting, often 45–90m long and 3–5m deep, with corks at the top and lead weights attached to the bottom. It is often fitted with a rope at each end of the cork-line to assist setting. It is not suitable for most running or heavily weeded waters, and will only work sucessfully where the net is deeper than the water (*ie* where the lead-line trails on the bottom).

The net is usually set in a semi-circle from a small boat as shown in *Figure 21*. The cork-lines are gently hauled in and slack on the lead-lines is taken up. Too strong a pull on the cork-line will cause the lead-line to rise clear of the bottom. When a small area remains, the lead-lines are pulled in until all are on the bank; the fish are thus trapped in the bag formed by the net. They can then be removed with long-handled landing nets and placed in keep nets or in tubs of aerated water. On long narrow waters, the net can be set across the water and 'walked' down to one end.

Netting problems occur when:

- The net catches on a snag: it can usually be freed by the man in the boat pulling it upwards from directly above the snag.
- Excessive amounts of silt are dragged in: this can be overcome by 'rocking' the silt-laden net before trying to remove the fish, but this can also damage the trapped fish.
- The water's edge may become boggy: it is wise always to wear thigh waders and select netting sites carefully.
- The net will not 'set' smoothly because of sticks and other débris left in the mesh from previous nettings: they should be removed and the net thoroughly cleaned with water after each netting. It may help if a large sheet of heavy-duty plastic is laid on the bank at the water's edge, and the net is placed on this as it is hauled.

It may be useful to carry out a series of seine nettings around a pond or lake. Furthermore, when there is the chance of a large number of fish being frightened out of the netting area, a second seine net can be set and left as a 'stop net' to prevent this. Seine netting should only be carried out after permission has been granted from the relevant regional Water Authority.

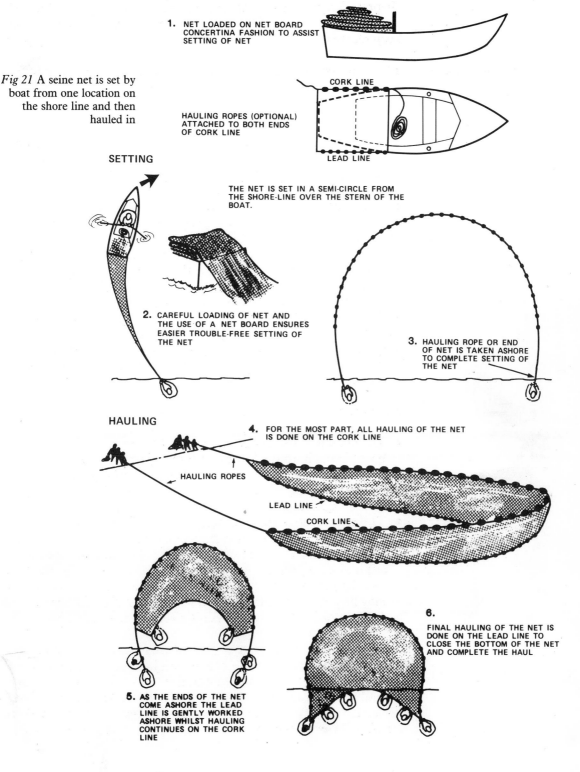

1. NET LOADED ON NET BOARD CONCERTINA FASHION TO ASSIST SETTING OF NET

Fig 21 A seine net is set by boat from one location on the shore line and then hauled in

CORK LINE

HAULING ROPES (OPTIONAL) ATTACHED TO BOTH ENDS OF CORK LINE

LEAD LINE

SETTING

THE NET IS SET IN A SEMI-CIRCLE FROM THE SHORE-LINE OVER THE STERN OF THE BOAT.

2. CAREFUL LOADING OF NET AND THE USE OF A NET BOARD ENSURES EASIER TROUBLE-FREE SETTING OF THE NET

3. HAULING ROPE OR END OF NET IS TAKEN ASHORE TO COMPLETE SETTING OF THE NET

HAULING

4. FOR THE MOST PART, ALL HAULING OF THE NET IS DONE ON THE CORK LINE

HAULING ROPES

LEAD LINE

CORK LINE

6. FINAL HAULING OF THE NET IS DONE ON THE LEAD LINE TO CLOSE THE BOTTOM OF THE NET AND COMPLETE THE HAUL

5. AS THE ENDS OF THE NET COME ASHORE THE LEAD LINE IS GENTLY WORKED ASHORE WHILST HAULING CONTINUES ON THE CORK LINE

41

Electric fishing

Electric fishing is an excellent means of capturing fish, but is not normally available to angling clubs. The technique is prohibited under the Salmon and Freshwater Fisheries Act 1975, but can be used under certain circumstances providing prior written permission is obtained from the Water Authority.

Most electric fishing operations will only catch fish in waters less than about 2m deep and less than 10m wide. They are thus not suited to fish capture in many ponds and lakes, although the use of stop nets may overcome these problems to some extent.

Fig 22 Direct and/or alternating current generators with control boxes and electrodes are used in electric fishing

The basis of the technique (*see Fig 22*) is that the current produced by a generator (or battery) is fed into the water by means of two or more electrodes, thereby creating an electrical field in the water. Electrical fishing techniques can be sub-divided into two types; alternating current (AC) which stuns the fish in its path, and direct current systems (DC) which induce fish to swim to the anode. In each case, the stunned fish can be removed from the water by hand nets and placed in tanks or keep nets to recover.

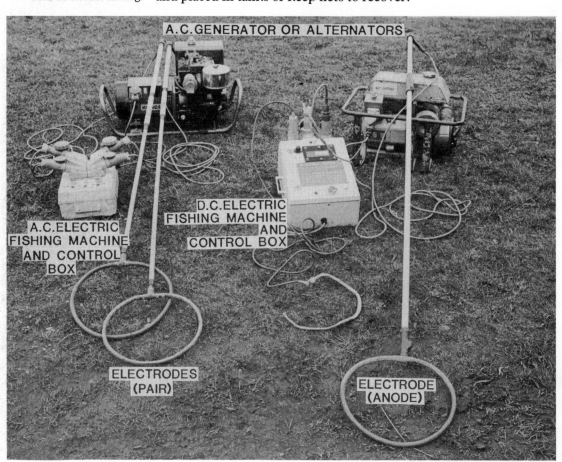

A.C. GENERATOR OR ALTERNATORS

A.C. ELECTRIC FISHING MACHINE AND CONTROL BOX

D.C. ELECTRIC FISHING MACHINE AND CONTROL BOX

ELECTRODES (PAIR)

ELECTRODE (ANODE)

AC systems are generally used in clear, unobstructed water, whereas DC is used in turbid, overgrown or weedy waters. Too strong a current, prolonged exposure to the field, or contact with the electrodes can kill fish or cause damage which later proves fatal. Electrical fishing is also potentially dangerous to the operators, and for this reason sophisticated safety devices are incorporated into the system, and a strict code of conduct should be enforced during all operations.

Angling

Angling (*Fig 23*) is often ignored as a sampling technique but can be one of the most useful methods of capturing fish. In particular, angling is one of the few methods of adequately sampling large lakes or deep, fast-flowing rivers. Catches may, however, be biased in favour of certain sizes or species of fish, depending upon the techniques used.

Fig 23 When all other methods fail, samples of fish can often be obtained from anglers fishing in a competition

The necessary information can be obtained directly from the fish as they are captured, or they may be retained in knotless nets until the fishing session is finished. Angling is commonly used in conjunction with mark–recapture studies, described later in this chapter.

'Drain-offs'

The removal of water (*Fig 24*) is an excellent technique for capturing fish but it is rarely practical because it is so expensive. The capital cost of hiring or purchasing pumps is high, and the cost of the fuel they consume may be considerable.

Pumping can be used to strand fish or to concentrate them into an area or enclosure from which they can then be removed by seine netting or by hand. A total drain-off can yield very precise data on the total numbers and weight of fish (the 'standing crop') present. Local fishery byelaws often stipulate that permission is needed to capture fish legally by the removal of water, and it is wise to consult the local Water Authority before undertaking any drain-off or draw-down work. The effect on other aquatic life is generally considered to be minimal provided that there is a local source of water to refill the pond or lake soon after completion of the operation.

Fig 24 The removal of water, drain-off, is a useful technique for capturing fish for examination or counting the total population

Other techniques

There are several other techniques (*see Fig 25*) which may be used to obtain fish samples, although most require either expensive equipment or are impractical in many fisheries. The nature of the fishery

44

and the type and extent of data required will determine which technique is most suitable, but it would be prudent to seek specialist advice before sampling begins.

Gill nets rely on the fact that fish will swim into a wall of fine net which is either suspended from the water surface or anchored to the bed of the fishery. The mesh size has a major influence in determining the size of fish caught, and most sampling will involve using 'gangs' of different sizes of gill nets. Fish mortality rates in gill nets are generally high, and they are therefore often used only to remove unwanted species (*eg* pike) from a fishery. They may also catch species which it is desired to retain. Gill nets are rarely employed in running water.

Trapping is a long-established fish capture technique and many styles of trap exist. Most traps include some form of leader which encourages fish encountering it to enter a central holding chamber. Permanently installed traps include those for migratory fish such as salmon, and can be designed around man-made fish deflectors such as the weirs used for capturing eels. Portable traps include hoop and fyke nets, and 'Windermere' perch traps.

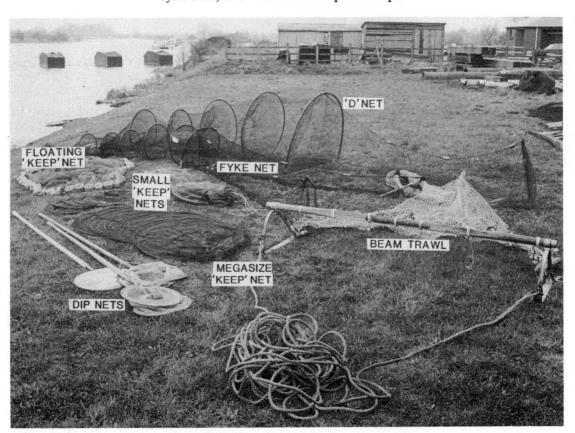

Fig 25 Various nets are available to sample and/or hold fish samples

Trawling is essentially a marine technique that has been scaled down and adapted for sampling large freshwaters. The mouth of an otter trawl is kept open by floats, weights and otter boards which act like underwater kites, whereas beam trawls are built on a rigid frame. They may be fished on the bottom or in midwater, and are often used in conjunction with echosounder or sonar equipment. Trawls have become widely used in some areas for sampling young fish in large lakes and reservoirs.

Poisoning is often used to achieve a total fish kill prior to fishery renovation. At sub-lethal levels, it can also be a successful method of sampling fish, although considerable care is needed in applying the correct dose of poison, and speed is essential when removing the narcotized fish. The most popular poison is rotenone, a natural plant derivative, and there is considerable scope for the development of less expensive and more easily applied alternatives, such as antimycin-A. Poisons are rarely specific in their action and may act on animals other than fish (including man!). As they are a prohibited fish capture technique under the Salmon and Freshwater Fisheries Act 1975, they must never be considered for use without first consulting the relevant Water Authority. Indeed, special consent of the Ministry of Agriculture, Fisheries and Food must be obtained by the Water Authority before they can be used by anybody.

Population estimates Following the capture of fish, it is often possible to make some estimate or calculation of the total size of the fish population. One of the most useful measures that can be made is of the weight of fish that a unit area of water contains. This is called the standing crop. Many waters hold 250–400kg of fish per hectare, although some will support less than this amount. If suitable habitat improvement techniques are applied, it may be possible to elevate this figure to 500, or even to 650kg/ha. There are three main techniques for estimating population numbers:

Direct counting

Where all the fish have been captured from a water, for instance following a 'drain-off' (*Fig 24*) it is a simple matter to count and weigh the fish.

Depletion technique

Where data are available from two or more successive samplings it is possible to estimate the total population size. This is only true if; (a) the same technique is applied to the same area each time, and (b) the catch on each occasion is smaller than that of the previous occasion.

46

If two successive samplings have been carried out,

and C_1 is the number of fish caught in Catch 1
and C_2 is the number of fish caught in Catch 2

then the population estimate (N) is calculated as

$$N = C_1^2/C_1 - C_2$$

This is the simplest type of depletion equation: there are many more complicated versions. The weight of fish present can be calculated by multiplying the estimated number by the average weight of the fish caught.

Mark–recapture techniques

The basis of any mark–recapture technique is that a known number of fish are taken, marked in some way (*see Fig 26*), and released. A subsequent sample of fish from the fishery should, if large enough, include some marked and some unmarked fish. The calculation of the population size can be made using various equations, one of the simplest of which is:

$$N = (M \times C)/R$$

Where N = population estimate
M = number of marked fish in population
C = total number of fish caught in second sample
R = number of marked fish recaptured in second sample

The ability to recognise fish because of individual characteristics, tags or marks is most useful. With experience, many individual fish can be identified by their colour and scale pattern, or because of deformities and scars. However, tagging or marking techniques give

Fig 26 There are several methods available for identifying individual fish

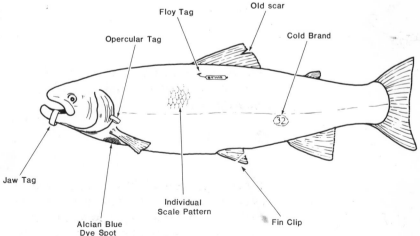

Fig 27 Fish can be marked or tagged for later identification with a variety of equipment

a more reliable and easily recognised method of identification. Several different methods of tagging and marking are shown in *Figure 27*.

Marking Of the various marking techniques used, the injection of 'alcian blue' dye is the most commonly used and the most successful. A solution of the dye is injected into the skin beneath a scale (or scales) by using either a syringe (usually a 1ml or 2ml disposable plastic syringe with a 23G or 25G needle) or a 'Panjet' inoculator. This instrument propels into the fish, at high pressure, a small volume of the liquid held within its reservoir. It is a dental instrument which requires minor modification by the manufacturer to enable it to be used for fish marking, but although expensive, it is both fast and safe in use.

The alcian blue can be injected to mark and identify batches of fish by using a common marking position on their bodies such as between the pectoral fins. Individual fish recognition can be achieved by using a combination of a series of marking sites. Alcian blue marks fade, however, and are generally lost after 1–2 years, although records exist of fish that have retained marks for 7 years.

48

Tags

Many different types of tags are used in fisheries biology, and each is suited to a particular need or species. Most are metal or plastic discs or tubes that are wired onto the gill covers or fin roots. They may bear a numbered code which enables the identification of individual fish.

Fin clips

The clipping or cutting away of part of a fin or fins is a popular method of marking fish. Cut fins will eventually regenerate, but evidence of the cut usually remains. Clipping sometimes affects the mobility of fish, and is best restricted to the paired fins or the adipose fin of salmonids.

Stock control When population estimate figures have been calculated, additions or removals to the stock of fish can be considered.

Fish stocking

It should be stressed that fish stocking should only be undertaken after other means of increasing the standing crop (*eg* habitat improvement) have been considered. In many situations a great deal of money has been wasted by introducing fish to fisheries where their chances of survival were poor, or where there was no need to supplement the existing natural stock of fish. Stocking is usually only necessary when there is a deficiency in natural reproduction; where the species has been reduced or eliminated; or where the species has not existed before and where conditions are suitable for that species.

The stocking of fish should be undertaken in a carefully planned manner. The type of species used will depend on the nature of the water to be stocked, and the type of fish required. It has been shown that stillwater fish may undertake a high degree of migration when stocked into rivers, thus providing very limited benefit to catches. Where possible, running waters should be stocked with fish that have originated from running water. Fish for re-stocking can be transferred from other waters, purchased from fish farmers, or sometimes obtained from the Water Authority. Even if it was originally devoid of fish, there is rarely justification for stocking a water with more than 300kg/ha of fish.

Before restocking occurs, it is necessary to obtain prior written permission from the Water Authority who often require a sample of the fish to ensure that they are not heavily diseased or parasitized.

Fish removal

The removal of unwanted or surplus fish can be achieved by using the capture techniques described earlier. In some cases it is possible to sell these fish to commercial fish suppliers, and the funds so raised can be used for other fishery development purposes. If it is not possible or practical to remove fish yourself, most fish suppliers will undertake this service although they will obviously pay a lower price for the fish so obtained. Alternatively, the Water Authority's Fisheries Department sometimes considers removing unwanted fish.

Keeping records The compiling and retention of an accurate set of records is an important aspect of good fisheries management. The fishery manager should keep detailed information on stocking dates, species and numbers of fish caught, *etc*. If angling competitions are held on the fishery, a complete record of the match results should be retained. Numbers of each species caught are most useful, in addition to total weights obtained by each competitor. This will enable past performance to be compared with present, and will give a good indication of any decline or improvement in the fishery. Photographic prints and slides are a means of recording physical features and provide useful additional information to that obtained from maps and depth charts.

Any information that is collected should be stored in an orderly, readily-accessible form, and should always include the date on which the information was collected.

1.7 Fish mortality

Fish, like any other living organism, are not immortal. To the angler, dead fish are often a cause for concern, but it must be remembered that in order to recycle the nutrients within them, the process of death and decomposition is essential for new life.

The premature death of fish can, of course, destroy a fishery, and the appearance of dead fish is often the first obvious sign of a polluting discharge that can threaten other animals or water supplies. The principal causes of mortality are summarized in *Figure 28*.

Causes attributable to man

Pollution

The main types of pollution have been described earlier. Generally, pollution only causes a fish mortality if it is sudden. An example is the sudden influx of a quantity of silage or piggery waste into a clean watercourse. If the pollution becomes continuous, fish may be eradicated, become accustomed to it, or migrate to unaffected areas, depending upon the volume, its strength and the extent of dilution afforded by the stream.

Angler-caused damage

Angling practices can, to a lesser or greater extent, physically damage fish. Hook damage to the mouth is a common injury, but foul-hooking can cause injuries almost anywhere on the body. Minor damage may be limited to the loss of a few scales, but this can nevertheless

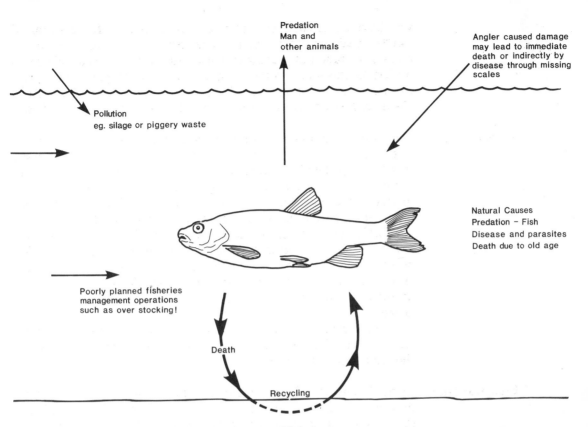

Predation
Man and
other animals

Angler caused damage
may lead to immediate
death or indirectly by
disease through missing
scales

Pollution
eg. silage or piggery waste

Natural Causes
Predation – Fish
Disease and parasites
Death due to old age

Poorly planned fisheries
management operations
such as over stocking!

Death

Recycling

Fig 28 Several causes of fish death

open the way for organisms like fungi and bacteria to gain entry to the fish.

The retention of fish in keep nets sometimes cause subcutaneous haemorrhages, split fins, and loss of protective mucus. The damage may be so severe that fish die as a result, or become infected with lethal diseases or parasites.

Catching fish by any method 'stresses' the fish. Such stress can alter the internal balance of body chemicals and make the fish more susceptible to disease. Stress cannot be avoided but it can, with careful and thoughtful angling practices, be kept to a minimum.

Fisheries management

Poorly-planned fisheries management operations can cause fish mortalities. There are many examples of how well-stocked and balanced fish populations have been altered by an unnecessary restocking operation, the extra stock causing stress, starvation and a decline in the fishery with the end result being poor fishing.

Natural causes　There are three main natural causes of death in fish: predation,

51

diseases and/or parasites, and old age. It should be borne in mind that fish compensate for these losses by producing far more eggs than could normally survive as adults, and that death from these causes is the method by which fish populations are naturally controlled.

Predation occurs at all stages of the life-cycle. The eggs and alevins of many fish are eaten by invertebrates like caddis-fly and beetle larvae, and by vertebrate animals such as frogs, birds, various mammals and adult fish. It has been calculated that a 97% mortality in roach from egg to fry was attributable to invertebrate predators, and that of 1·5 million pike eggs in a river population, only 68 fish survived to become large enough to be caught on rod and line.

Many coarse fish fry will also die if the right food is not available at the correct period in their development. The fish which survive these young stages are still subject to predation from other fish and animals, but the older and larger they become, the lower the risk from predation.

Disease and parasites

Fish diseases usually act in conjunction with other environmental factors: stress is particularly important in causing outbreaks. This can happen with a change in water quality which lasts for a considerable time but which is not in itself sufficient to kill fish. It may be stressful enough, however, to make the fish more susceptible to resident disease organisms. Hence, significant fluctuations in the levels of DO, temperature, pH, ammonia, salinity, suspended solids and others may all cause stressful conditions.

Many diseases and parasites (*Fig 29*) are common on fish farms. Poor husbandry techniques can soon lead to severe outbreaks which, if left untreated, can cause large mortalities. Most fish farmers are familier with the basic diagnostic and treatment techniques, but the best cure for disease on the fish farm is to prevent them occurring in the first place by ensuring that good husbandry techniques are practised.

Examples of large mortalities in the wild are fortunately not common, and most fish will carry a complement of parasites without any untoward effect. There are examples, however, of infestations that have killed or damaged individual fish or whole populations, and they commonly occur in overcrowded fisheries.

Tapeworms like *Ligula* sp. (*see Fig 29*) take food from their host and they may also render it infertile. Other tapeworms block the gut and cause fish to die through a lack of nutrients. Skin parasites can irritate the fish and cause considerable damage to the skin. Wounds caused by parasites often allow the entry of secondary bacterial and fungal infections, and these can frequently lead to the death of the fish. The fish louse, for example, often causes severe skin damage

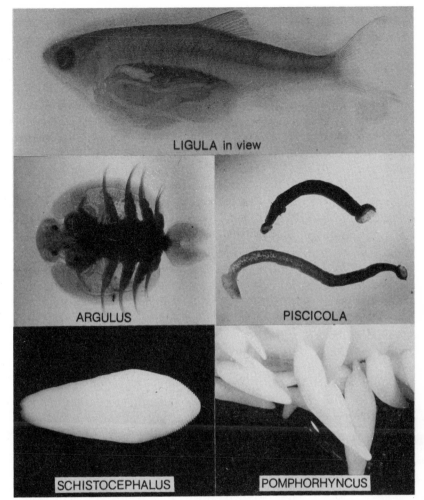

LIGULA in view

ARGULUS

PISCICOLA

SCHISTOCEPHALUS

POMPHORHYNCUS

Fig 29 Some of the common parasites on freshwater fish

which can become infected, and coupled with the toxin the parasite injects, can prove fatal.

Despite all these hazards it is possible that some fish do, in fact, die of old age, although the exact meaning of this term is the subject of much speculation.

Poor condition Many anglers are able to recognize when a fish is in good or poor condition (*Fig 30*). It is possible to calculate the relative 'fitness' of a fish by relating its weight to its length, and this condition factor gives a clue to the healthiness or otherwise of the individual or population.

Most fish populations contain the occasional fish in poor condition, and such specimens are usually found to carry a higher than normal parasite load, or be physically damaged and so unable to feed properly. However, reports of large numbers of poorly conditioned fish from the same water should always be investigated as they are usually symptomatic of one of many fisheries management problems.

53

Fig 30 An example of a trout in poor condition

Poor flesh taste Complaints are occasionally received that fish taste unpleasant when eaten. It is difficult to evaluate the taste of fish flesh objectively. Towner Coston *et al* in their book *River Management* in 1936 said that, 'flavour is very largely a question of personal opinion, *eg* some people declare that River Test trout are uneatable, others that they are as good as any other trout.' The flesh of any animal is often only as good as the food that the animal has eaten, and it is possible that a trout can take on the flavour of the invertebrates it has been eating. If those invertebrates have themselves consumed certain types of plankton, then this may result in a poor taste. There appears to be very little the fisheries manager can do about this. Sometimes, however, fish flesh can become tainted due to very small quantities of chemicals such as phenols, which have contaminated the water.

Part 2: Management techniques and methods

Part 1 of this book has described the resource that the fishery manager is expected to manage. It is now time to consider some of the techniques available to him. A decision will have to be made at a fairly early stage as to the objectives of management action, and efforts should be made to determine whether or not it is possible to attain those objectives. It is pointless, for instance, deciding that a fishery should be managed for large carp if anglers do not want to fish for them!

Depending on how they are managed, all fisheries can be categorized in some way. Natural fisheries, by definition, are not managed. The species present are known only from past catches, and no restocking, destocking or habitat improvement operations are undertaken. The facilities may, however, have been improved for the angler. Examples include most of the mixed coarse fisheries of the River Trent and the River Thames, and many salmon rivers. Specialist fisheries are those in which an angler expects to catch a certain target species. These fisheries are intensively managed, nearly always stocked, and have been subject to habitat improvement works. Examples include put-and-take salmonid fisheries and specialist carp fisheries. Somewhere between these two fall all other fisheries.

2.1 Management of coarse fisheries

All the natural and semi-natural coarse fisheries contain some or all of the species mentioned in section 1.4. The techniques used to manage these fisheries exploit their natural biological and physical requirements.

Main biological groups of coarse fish

Coarse fish can be split into four main biological groups.

- The requirements of the first group (bream, carp and tench) are similar. The adults live in slow-flowing rivers, or lakes that are normally warm. The fish are predominantly shoal members, and spawn in spring or early summer at temperatures varying from 16°C (for bream) to 20–22°C (for carp and tench). The eggs are normally deposited on weed or reed beds, and although the fish

55

spawn in shoals, the eggs are scattered fairly diffusely over the weeds so that some escape predation. The eggs hatch after a week or so, and the fry feed during hours of daylight on the early summer zooplankton. They grow quickly during the warm months and form large shoals at this time. The fish normally mature after three or four years. In the case of carp there are a number of different scale patterns and body forms, and king carp, common carp and mirror carp are all the same species.

- The second group of fish comprises the mid-river cyprinids such as barbel, dace and chub. These fish are naturally absent from stillwaters but can live in reservoirs if accidentally introduced. They differ significantly from the carp and tench group in their temperature requirements. They spawn from March (in the case of dace) until June (for chub and barbel) at temperatures of 10–13°C. The preferred spawning substrate is gravelly shallows, and the eggs can take up to 25 days to hatch at 13°C. The fry are longer and thinner than carp or tench fry and can measure up to 7·5mm. Maturity occurs after two or three years. A good deal of vegetable matter is contained in the diet, and chub can also eat a great range of scavenged matter as well as small fish and crayfish.

- The third group consists of gudgeon, stoneloach and bullhead, of which the gudgeon is quite important in fisheries such as the Trent and Soar rivers. They are all bottom-living fish and eat benthic invertebrates such as chironomid larvae and molluscs. Spawning takes place in April–May in dense shoals, and the sticky eggs are shed onto plants and stones. They take up to two weeks to hatch and growth rate is fast over three to four years, but slows thereafter. The biggest fish of this type are around 15cm, but they are usually much smaller.

- The fourth group contains the predators – pike, perch and zander. These are all carnivorous in habit, although the young stages take members of the zooplankton. Older pike and zander eat mainly fish, but perch eat a more varied diet of small fish, crustaceans, beetles and worms. Perch and zander form shoals to locate and catch their prey, but pike are more solitary hunters. Pike and perch spawn as early as February through to April in shallow areas, on last year's reed beds; perch spawn after pike and leave very characteristic ribbons of eggs around reed stems; zander spawn from April to June at temperatures around 15°C, and the eggs are shed in shallow water on reed or rush stems.
Pike and zander grow large, pike reaching 20kg and zander reaching 8kg. Perch are smaller fish – seldom exceeding 2kg when mature.

Specialist coarse fisheries   There appears to be an increasing demand by anglers for specialist coarse fisheries. They therefore need to be biologically productive

56

and the chosen species stocked at a low initial density to allow for growth. To maintain a fishery of this type, regular cropping of any progeny from the initial stocking of fish must be undertaken in order to reduce competition for food and create conditions for growth. Two examples of specialist fisheries are those managed for carp and for pike.

Carp

Carp (*Fig 31*) were originally introduced into Britain several hundred years ago. Because their natural range is in areas of warmer summer climate, British water temperatures seldom reach the optimum for growth of this species (around 25°C). For this reason carp normally grow faster in shallow lakes than in deeper colder lakes. However, an ideal carp pool should have some deeper areas as well as shallow ones, since deeper water will buffer the effects of sudden changes in temperature.

The pool that is to be developed as a carp fishery will probably already contain a mixed fish population. The first step is to remove the unwanted coarse fish, and to do this properly, the pool should be drained either by lowering via a sluice or 'monk' (if present), or by pumping.

It is wise to restock the pool with only about 150–250kg/ha of carp in order to allow for growth. If the pool was not very productive initially, fertilization should be undertaken to improve the productivity. If, after fertilization, the pool is capable of supporting 600kg of fish per hectare, the young fish of successive spawnings will quickly grow to achieve the maximum biomass the pool can support. Annual or bi-annual cropping of small carp may then be necessary if good growth rates are to be maintained.

Pike

The same basic techniques are required to produce a specimen pike fishery (*Fig 32*). The pool should be fertilized to provide a high standing crop of prey fish which in turn will support a high standing crop of pike. Although carp fisheries can be developed in small waters, pools larger than about 3ha are needed to produce the level of stock that will support a specialist pike fishery.

The main problem with a pike fishery is in trying to achieve the correct balance between pike and prey fish. Pike often live in balance with a prey fish population when the weight-for-weight ratio is 1:7 or 1:8 – that is, 1kg of pike for every 8kg of prey fish, although there is evidence that balance can be achieved even at ratios as far apart as 1:4 and 1:20. Obviously the lower ratio is more advantageous to pike fishermen since any water stocked in this way will contain more pike. It should be borne in mind that a specialist pike fishery should, if managed correctly, also produce big fish of the prey species. The type of prey introduced can be determined by the type of fishing required

57

Fig 31 A fine specimen-sized carp weighing 7.0kg   *Fig 32* Two specimen-sized pike, each weighing 10.0kg

and in larger waters the prey fish stocks could comprise a mixture of bream, roach and perch.

Once the fishery has been created great care must be exercised in managing it. Because the fish are likely to be caught several times it may be necessary to persuade anglers to use tackle and tactics that cause the least damage to the pike they catch (barbless hooks, knotless nets, minimum line strengths). Similarly, in order to further protect the stocks, the angler effort and use of the fishery may also have to be carefully controlled lest the accidental death of some of the fish leads to a deterioration in sport. When stocks are lost, additional replacement fish will be required. Stock fish can often be obtained if contact is made with angling clubs who wish to remove unwanted pike.

2.2 Management of salmonid fisheries

Five species of salmonids form breeding populations in the British Isles. Three – the Atlantic salmon, brown trout and char – are native to this country; two – the rainbow trout and American brook trout – were introduced in the last century and have established self-sustaining populations at a few locations. The fishery manager can gain some idea of the suitability of his water for and the biological requirements of these species from *Table 2*. There are some specific management techniques for still and running waters which contain salmonids. These techniques may be conveniently divided into indirect or direct.

58

Requirement	Salmon-river stage	Brown trout (BT)	Rainbow trout	American brook trout
Preferred growth temperature °C	13–15	12	14	12–14
Normal maximum temperature	16–17	19	20–21	19
Spawning temperature °C	0–8	2–10	4–10	2–10
Normal spawning times	November–December	November–December	November	Sept-November
Size of spawning gravel	3–16cm	1–5cm	1–5cm	1–5cm
Egg size	5–7mm	3–6mm	approx 5mm	3–6mm
No. of eggs per kg of adult body weight	1 100–2 000	1 100–2 600	1 100–2 600	approx 2 800
Incubation period	88 days at 5°C	40 days at 10°C	32 at 10°C	85 days at 7°C
pH range	5–9	5–9	5–9	4.5–9.5
DO requirements	>5mg/l^{-1} best at 9mg/l^{-1}	>5mg/l^{-1} best at 9mg/l^{-1}	4–4.5mg/l^{-1} best at 9mg/l^{-1}	4–4.5mg/l^{-1} best at 9mg/l^{-1}
Feeding requirements	Similar to BT but feed more often on surface and live in faster water	Feed on bottom animals, in mid-water and on surface	Similar to BT – thought to feed over a wider temp. range	Feeds in mid-water and from surface and at lower temp. than BT

Indirect methods

Increased spawning escapement

This is often achieved by a fishery authority imposing a legal restriction on where and when adult fish can be caught. Such restrictions give a greater chance for the adult salmon to escape capture and move into their spawning river.

Kelt conservation

Mortality in salmon kelts (fish that have spawned) can be as high as 95%, and their contribution as repeat spawners is therefore not significant. Kelt conservation, even though traditionally accepted, is of very limited value for most rivers.

Improved water quality

Effective programmes of national and river catchment pollution control can be the greatest single contributory factor in the improvement of salmon stocks. Locally, the prevention of pollution accidents should be a priority for fishery owner, lessee and Water Authority in order to protect spawning gravels and juvenile populations.

Increased spawning areas

Poor accessibility to spawning grounds due to man-made or natural obstructions can be improved through the provision of better passage facilities. Advice should be sought from the local fishery or Regional Water Authority.

Other improvements to existing spawning areas may include some of those techniques discussed elsewhere in this book, including the prevention of siltation, removal of predators, and control of afforestation. Afforestation tends to slow or decrease drainage, whilst deforestation results in an increase in flood and low water flows.

Direct methods   Direct methods of stock improvement employ the collection of eggs, their fertilization and subsequent planting out as ova or unfed fry, or rearing on to the fed fry, parr or smolt stage. Traditionally, the direct method has been the acceptable practice for salmon improvement. However, it has been shown that ultimately the carrying capacity of the river is the controlling factor. It therefore follows that the yield of parr and smolts from a stocked river is not significantly different from that of an unstocked river. A higher number of adult fish return if a river is stocked with smolts reared in a hatchery – an exercise that avoids the usual high mortality of the fry and parr stages.

If planting out of ova or fry is necessary in order to increase the salmon run, it must be on a large enough scale to produce measurable results. The direct method is justified in the following cases:

- Where rearing to parr or smolt stage is part of a compensation scheme when, for example, a reservoir or power station is constructed, presenting a complete barrier to upstream spawning fish.
- When planting of eggs, fry or parr follows loss due to accidental pollution.
- When re-establishing a run in a river system following water quality improvement.

Table 3 RECOMMENDED STOCKING RATES FOR SALMON EGGS AND FRY

Green ova, eyed ova, unfed fry	200–600/100m^2 (in batches of 1–2 000)
Fed fry	100–300/100m^2
1+ parr	40–120/100m^2
2+ parr	5–15/100m^2

In circumstances where rearing is necessary, every effort should be made to obtain suitable parent stock, either from the same river or the adjacent catchment area in order to maintain genetic adaptations to the local environment. The carrying capacity of a stream is governed largely by the shape of the bed and banks, although with the methods of physical habitat improvement described in Section 2.6, this capacity can be increased.

Management techniques for flowing water salmonids fall into two categories; natural fisheries and artificial fisheries.

Natural or self-sustaining fisheries   On rivers that support a natural trout population (normally brown trout in the British Isles), the anglers represent an additional predator upon the larger and older component of the trout population.

60

Successful management requires the regulation of the anglers to prevent over-exploitation of the potential brood stock. Regulatory measures include the restriction of the number of rod days, bag limits, size limits and angling methods. The successful control and management of a natural trout fishery also depends upon obtaining complete and honest catch returns from all anglers.

Artificial or maintained fisheries

In river trout fisheries that are not able to support the fishing pressure imposed upon them, it is necessary to supplement the natural production of takeable trout by stocking. Artificial fisheries may also be created to provide trout fishing in rivers that do not have a resident trout population, or to provide variety in species or size which the natural population does not contain.

Choice of species is limited to brown and rainbow trout, as American brook trout are very rarely stocked in rivers in Britain owing to their strong tendency to migrate considerable distances. Brown trout is the most widely used species in artificial river fisheries because it is the most naturally suitable. Furthermore, anglers who habitually fish rivers seem to prefer brown trout. Historically, rainbow trout have been regarded as generally unsuitable for river fisheries because of their tendency to migrate. However, in recent years they have become more widely accepted and are capable of providing economical and satisfactory sport.

As a general guideline, it is usually most effective and economical to stock with takeable sized fish. The introduction of eggs, fry or sub-legal fish on a stream with a low number of anglers and poor spawning facilities is possible but will not produce the consistent high-quality sport demanded by anglers from rivers that are heavily fished.

Stock fish are expensive, and careless handling of the stocking arrangements can lead to poor sport and financial loss. Any fish introduced in excess of the carrying capacity will rapidly migrate and be lost to the fishery. Experience has shown that in rivers such as the upper Severn and Teme catchments, between 5 and 20 takeable (in excess of 25cm) fish per 100m of stream may be expected. If it is decided that the carrying capacity of a particular 5km stream is 10 takeable trout per 100m, then the maximum number of takeable fish likely to be present at any one time is 500. If the expected total catch during a typical fishing season is 3 000 fish, considerable stocking is obviously necessary.

With all species of trout, stocking should be restricted to immediately before and during the fishing season. Wherever possible, the stocking rate should be adjusted to take account of the current performance of the fishery, with the object of maintaining the takeable population at its maximum level. As with the natural fisheries, good management depends on reliable angler catch returns, and stocking is best carried out just before the takeable population becomes so low as to reduce catches. Frequency of stocking depends on angling pressure and a flexible arrangement with the supplier of stock fish is desirable.

Towards the end of the season, stocking should be carefully monitored so that as few fish as possible remain in the stream at the end of the season. If a few brown trout remain uncaught, this may be of benefit as spawning is possible. Rainbow trout that are not caught before the end of the season represent a complete loss to the fishery as they are extremely unlikely to spawn successfully and may migrate downstream during winter high flows.

When it is considered necessary to introduce fish, stocking large batches at boundaries should be avoided as stock fish disperse out of the stocked area.

Stillwater salmonid fisheries With the possible exception of char, salmonids rarely breed successfully in stillwaters unless there is a suitable inflowing stream or streams. Most lowland trout lakes are therefore stocked on a 'put-and-take' basis. Rainbow trout are more tolerant than brown trout of higher water temperatures and lower oxygen concentrations. Under similar conditions, rainbow trout tend to grow faster than brown trout, and shallower alkaline lakes produce the best growth for both species. The lifespan and overwinter survival is usually lower for rainbow trout than brown trout but, even so, recapture rates for rainbow trout are often greater than those for brown trout, relative to numbers stocked. Because of these differences, and the individual preferences of anglers, most fisheries are stocked with a mixture of brown and rainbow trout. (Work is currently being done to reduce overwinter losses using, for example, sterile or all female fish – *see Appendix 6.*)

There is a higher percentage return on numbers of fish introduced from spring-stocked fish than from autumn-stocked fish, and growth at lower winter temperatures is also unlikely. Frequent stocking with small numbers of fish throughout the season will also give a higher rate of return: sometimes 90% of all fish caught are taken within 45 days of being stocked.

Fishing pressure, and the demands of anglers for large 'wild-type' fish, may result in some variations in stocking policy. The regular stocking of a small proportion of comparatively large farm-reared trout, for example, may often give a better return to the angler seeking the 'unexpected' large fish than relying on fish that may have survived from one season to the next. Most trout that are left uncaught at the end of the fishing season in stillwater fisheries can be regarded as a wasted resource. It is therefore important that up-to-date records be kept of the numbers of fish stocked, and those recaptured, in order that consideration can be given, for example, to changes in the permitted methods of fishing towards the end of the season. This will help to reduce this waste and maximize exploitation.

The actual stocking density varies from water to water. A per hectare per year stocking rate of 50 to 80 fish when using trout between 25 and 30cm is recommended for large lowland reservoirs. This is equivalent to an input of 10–15kg of fish/ha/yr. Many smaller 'put-and-take' trout fisheries use higher stocking rates. In rich water, up to 100kg of trout per hectare can obtain sufficient natural food to remain in good condition, if not grow in size; but in poorer waters a stocking density below 75kg of trout/ha (say 150 takeable fish) may be more advisable. Fishing will become difficult when the number of trout in a water drops to between 30 and 50 fish per hectare.

Waters fed by streams that provide spawning and nursery facilities typically contain a large population of stunted fish. A larger average-size fish can be obtained if the numbers of fish are reduced. This may be achieved by increased angling pressure coupled with the lowering or removal of size limits. Spawning barriers can also be used to prevent or restrict the movement of mature fish into inflowing streams. Alternatively, eggs and/or fry can be destroyed in nursery areas by the use of fish poisons such as rotenone.

There are further management techniques that can be used to create a new fishery or to improve an established one. The remainder of this section will describe some of these, and some techniques for maintaining the fishery.

2.3 Construction of stillwaters

There will be occasions when the only way to obtain a fishery is either to create an entirely new one, or to restore an existing pool. Anyone undertaking this work will need to take into account the many legal requirements which could apply (*see Appendix 5*).

Requirements for coarse fish pools

If it is intended that the pool be a coarse fishery, great water depths are not required; a good design would be one where one-third of the pond was less than 1m deep, one-third of medium depth (1–2m deep) and one-third 2–3m deep. Coarse fish generally favour warmer water than trout, and shallow waters are the most productive for food. Although there are advantages in having very shallow margins, they may not be fishable and it is better if these are dug out to 1–2m deep. This helps to prevent excessive growths of marginal vegetation and enables keep nets to be used. It also provides more water area for fishing. Where possible, the pool should have indented margins which will add more variety to the pool so that anglers may find sheltered spots, and will increase the bankside space available. Screening trees can also be planted (see Section 2.7).

Requirements for trout pools

In general terms, trout pools should be deeper than those described for coarse fishery. Trout do not thrive in temperatures in excess of 20°C, and in a hot summer this temperature may be exceeded in a shallow pool. An average depth of 2·5m is ideal, with some areas exceeding 3·5m. Shallow areas should be greater than 1m, and the margins should be relatively deep (1–2m), although this is not essential. Lakes of less than 0·5ha are not normally suitable for trout unless there is a flow-through of fresh water.

Excavation of a pond or lake is an expensive business so care should be exercised to ensure that the most economical equipment is used for the job. It is essential that the site is surveyed, and the depths determined, so that deep areas can be constructed where there is little soil to remove, and 'high spots' are left as shallows. It is a good idea to dig a few trial holes across the proposed bed of the lake to determine the nature of the bed before work begins.

If the pool is to be constructed 'off line', the land will probably lie some 1–1·5m above the adjacent watercourse, and the topsoil may be 0·3m thick, with underlying gravel. In such a case, it is likely that the height of the water table will be at river level and the excavation of this pool will be very expensive since it will be necessary to dig down 1–1·5m before the top water level is reached. It is also unlikely that the pool could be drained, which would make future management of the fishery much more difficult.

If the pool is to be constructed by damming a valley, then great care should be taken. A pool of average depth 2·5m and area 1·2ha impounds about 22·8 megalitres of water, and at this size and larger, the construction of the reservoir requires a 'Panel 1' civil engineer to supervise the design and construction. This can prove very costly. The economics indicate that unless a lake of nearly 4ha is required, it is better to confine the area to 1·2ha and/or the capacity to below 22·8 megalitres. If in doubt, seek the advice of a qualified engineer. (A 'Panel 1' civil engineer is one who, under the Reservoir (Safety Provisions) Act 1930, has been appointed by the Secretary of State to Panel 1 of the three Panels of Reservoir Inspectors.)

Construction of on-line pools There are several major points to remember when constructing a pool, some of which are shown in *Figure 33*.

If a pool is to be constructed on-line (that is with a stream flowing into it and overflowing out) it will be liable to silting and may require dredging after a number of years.

The overflow or spillway of the pool (*Fig 34*) should be wide enough to allow flood flows to pass over it to a depth of no more than 7·5cm. This will prevent loss of fish and will eliminate the need for gratings, which require regular cleaning. (Details of flood flows can be obtained from a Water Authority river engineer).

Calculation of spillway size

Method 1; for small ponds

If the highest river-bank marks left by a flood were 3m apart, measured from bank to bank, and the average depth of water during the flood was 0·5m, this is divided by 10cm (desired depth of flow) to

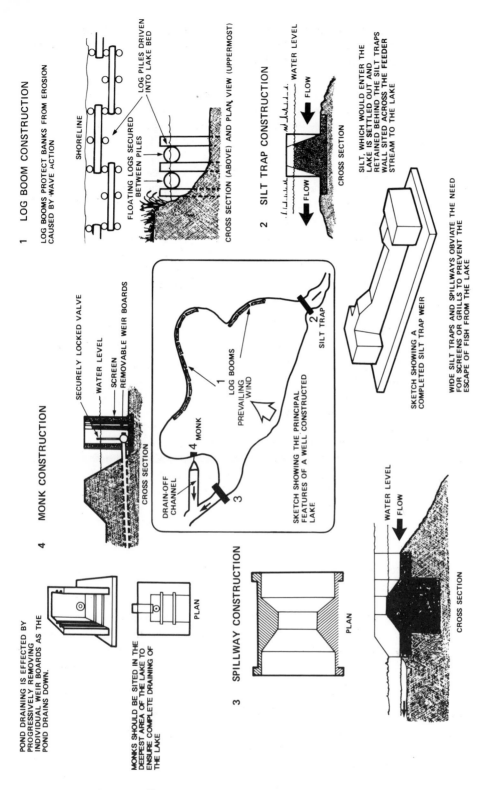

65

Fig 33 This diagram gives details of four features to be considered when constructing a lake

1 LOG BOOM CONSTRUCTION

LOG BOOMS PROTECT BANKS FROM EROSION CAUSED BY WAVE ACTION

SHORELINE

FLOATING LOGS SECURED BETWEEN PILES

LOG PILES DRIVEN INTO LAKE BED

CROSS SECTION (ABOVE) AND PLAN VIEW (UPPERMOST)

2 SILT TRAP CONSTRUCTION

WATER LEVEL

FLOW

FLOW

CROSS SECTION

SILT, WHICH WOULD ENTER THE LAKE IS SETTLED OUT AND RETAINED BEHIND THE SILT TRAPS WALL SITED ACROSS THE FEEDER STREAM TO THE LAKE

SKETCH SHOWING A COMPLETED SILT TRAP WEIR

WIDE SILT TRAPS AND SPILLWAYS OBVIATE THE NEED FOR SCREENS OR GRILLS TO PREVENT THE ESCAPE OF FISH FROM THE LAKE

4 MONK CONSTRUCTION

SECURELY LOCKED VALVE

WATER LEVEL

SCREEN

REMOVABLE WEIR BOARDS

CROSS SECTION

POND DRAINING IS EFFECTED BY PROGRESSIVELY REMOVING INDIVIDUAL WEIR BOARDS AS THE POND DRAINS DOWN.

MONKS SHOULD BE SITED IN THE DEEPEST AREA OF THE LAKE TO ENSURE COMPLETE DRAINING OF THE LAKE

PLAN

3 SPILLWAY CONSTRUCTION

PLAN

WATER LEVEL

FLOW

CROSS SECTION

SKETCH SHOWING THE PRINCIPAL FEATURES OF A WELL CONSTRUCTED LAKE.

1 LOG BOOMS

PREVAILING WIND

2 SILT TRAP

4 MONK

3

DRAIN-OFF CHANNEL

Fig 34 Photograph of a newly-constructed spillway

give a factor of 5. The 3m width is then multiplied by 5 to give a spillway width of 15m which will be sufficiently wide to handle water from a flood of the size estimated. This method works satisfactorily only if the drift deposits can be located along the stream banks, their height measured, and there is no obstruction downstream from the pond.

Method 2; for drainage areas of less than 20ha supplying a pond

The total number of hectares in the drainage catchment is divided by two to give an arbitrary spillway width in metres. To this is added a further 3m as a safety margin. If, for example, the drainage area of the pond is 11·2ha, this method will determine that the spillway should be 8·6m wide.

Method 3; for drainage areas of more than 50ha

The size of the spillway may be computed from the amount of 'run-off' from the drainage area. Specialist advice will be necessary to calculate this figure.

Location of spillway　Since most ponds are built in natural hollows, the spillway is often constructed on the dam. However, it may be located at one or both ends of the dam, or at a convenient point alongside the pond.

Spillway construction　The spillway should be paved with stone or concrete (*Fig 34*) to prevent erosion. The type of construction to use will depend on the location of the spillway, the type of soil on which it is to be built, and the amount of water it will have to carry. Regardless of the type of construction used, the spillway that is to cope with all overflow should be paved for a sufficient distance to carry the water away from the dam to avoid any erosion to it.

Diversion ditches　An on-line pool may be protected from flood flows by constructing a diversion ditch (*Fig 35*) around the pool. Once the design has been made and construction completed, the ditch should be seeded so that its grassed bed will reduce the eroding effect of the flood water. A diversion dam or sluice can then be constructed in the stream above the pool so that flood flows are forced around the pool and down the ditch. One suitable design might be an earth dam built across the stream and incorporating a pipe which would discharge into the pool and govern its supply. Alternatively, sluices could be sited in the stream in order to allow a supply to the pool, but enable this to be shut down in times of flood.

Fig 35 An on-line pool (middle ground) may be protected from flood flows by constructing a diversion ditch (foreground)

Erosion On large ponds, the wind often creates waves large enough to erode windward banks above and below water level. This action on new ponds may be so severe that a quarter of a metre or more of bank can be washed away in one day. A single log wall built along the bank at normal water level will absorb the impact of the wave's energy and prevent this erosion, as will a gently sloping bank lined with reeds. Logs 25–30cm in diameter and 6m long are placed in position along the face of the bank (*see Fig 33*) and stakes are driven into the bed at each side to hold them in place. The logs should be lapped so that there are no gaps between them. A system of this type allows a certain amount of fluctuation of water level whilst still maintaining good bank protection. Floating log booms (*Fig 36*) will reduce wave build-up across large stretches of open water.

On small ponds, a short-term solution is to place a good layer of

Fig 36 A floating boom constructed of logs chained together will reduce wave build-up across large stretches of water

68

turf on the face of the bank or dam to help prevent serious erosion by wave action.

Another method of reducing erosion is to drive willow stakes into the bank below water level and weave willow branches in and out of the stakes. The gap behind the stakes is then infilled with soil and either seeded or covered with turf. This method has the advantage that the willow stakes and branches will often grow, providing shelter and cover for fish.

Off-line pools Pools constructed off-line (*Fig 37*) do not usually suffer from the same silt problems as those on-line. The water supply to the pool can be obtained from a diversion channel, and the inflow may be controlled by a sluice or penstock at the junction of the brook, or by a small dam containing a pipe. Flood flows can safely pass down the brookcourse. A pool of this type will not require a large spillway, since flood flows will pass around it.

Fig 37 A pool constructed off-line, several feet below the level of the adjacent river

Silt trap construction

If the pool is fed by a stream, it is often desirable to build a wall across the stream to isolate an area near the inlet so that this will act as a silt trap (*Figs 33 and 38*). Alternatively, a small pool can be constructed in the stream upstream of the fishing pool, and this can be cleaned regularly to reduce siltation in the fishery itself. To be as effective as possible, the silt trap should have a long weir apron over which the water passes, as this slows the water velocity and prevents silt from being carried downstream.

Draining pools

If a stillwater fishery is to be managed correctly, it may be necessary periodically to remove unwanted fish stocks, and since pools decline in productivity as they age, it is also beneficial to leave them fallow occasionally.

There are several means of assisting pool drainage, and the simplest type, if the bed of the pond is higher in level than a convenient nearby stream, is a monk, named after monks who first devised the structures for their fish ponds (*see Figs 33 and 39*). A monk consists of a box containing a pipe at the bottom which drains the ponds. The depth of water is governed by stop-boards, which can be raised or lowered at will to control the height of the water in the pond. It is best to site the monk away from the bank so that it may only be reached by boat, as this will help prevent unauthorized tampering. If the monk is constructed of wood, timber such as pitch pine or elm should be used since they can withstand about 30 years immersion in water without rotting. Concrete collars can be used with concrete slabs as stop-logs if a more permanent structure is to be built.

Fig 38 A silt trap

Fig 39 A stone-built monk set several metres from the bank

Legal requirements The erection, alteration or repair of any structure in, over or under a watercourse may require consent from the Water Authority under the Land Drainage Act 1976 (*see* Appendix 5). The construction of a lake and filling of a lake with water from an adjoining watercourse may require a licence under the Water Resources Act and consent under the Land Drainage Act, and may also need planning consent from the Planning Authority. Informal discussions are often the best way of finding out whether legal consent is required. What may require formal approval in one area may be permitted without it in an adjoining area.

The design and construction of water-retaining structures is a skilled job requiring professional expertise. The failure of an impounding structure, even though it may retain only relatively small quantities of water, can have severe consequences and may put lives at risk. It is therefore recommended that the design and supervision of construction of impounding works be carried out by a qualified and experienced civil engineer. It is worth remembering that land suitable for creating a lake may not be under the same ownership as the watercourse itself.

71

2.4 Maintenance of stillwaters

Over a period of years there is a tendency for ponds to revert to marshland, but this process can be arrested if the silt that accumulates within them is removed. This is particularly true when there are large deposits of black, semi-decomposed leaf-litter and debris. This material will tend to reduce oxygen levels in the pond, and because it often produces acidic conditions it may also reduce the fertility of the pool. In pools that have become very shallow as a result of silt and organic debris, fish stocks may be at risk, mortalities may occur, and the maximum standing crop that can be sustained may be reduced.

Desilting techniques

Desilting a pool can prove costly, but costs can be significantly reduced if spoil can be deposited 'on site' rather than transported elsewhere. The silt removal exercise will be easier if the pond can be drained; on a pool such as a gravel pit without any monk or sluice arrangement, it may be possible to pump out the pool. This will depend on the permeability of the adjacent land and the proximity of water sources, but it enables the operator to see what he is doing, and the spoil is relatively dry and more easily handled. Care should be taken, however, to ensure that muddy water does not pollute watercourses downstream.

Types of machine and their limitations

The types of machine that can be used to desilt a pool (*Fig 40*) will vary from pool to pool according to local topography, strength of substrate, ease of access, bankside vegetation and a number of other factors – including cost.

Draglines

The dragline is the most common type of machine used for larger stillwaters, but it has limitations. It is rarely possible to use it from anywhere other than the bank, and the maximum reach that can be achieved is normally 20m, although a very large machine may be capable of reaching over 30m.

For safety reasons, draglines cannot operate within $1\frac{1}{4}$ jib lengths of an overhead power line, and they require a considerable clear area in which to swing the bucket and dump spoil. They cannot therefore be used on a pool surrounded by trees, unless some of these are removed. Draglines are usually delivered to the site on a large trailer which requires good access; they require a track width of at least 3·0m and because of their extreme weight, small bridges may not be able to accommodate them.

Hydraulic excavator

The reach of a hydraulic excavator is limited and this type of machine is not generally suitable for the majority of pools. On small pools that are surrounded by trees, however, this type of excavator may be the only practical means of removing silt. Larger machines can have jib lengths of over 12m reach.

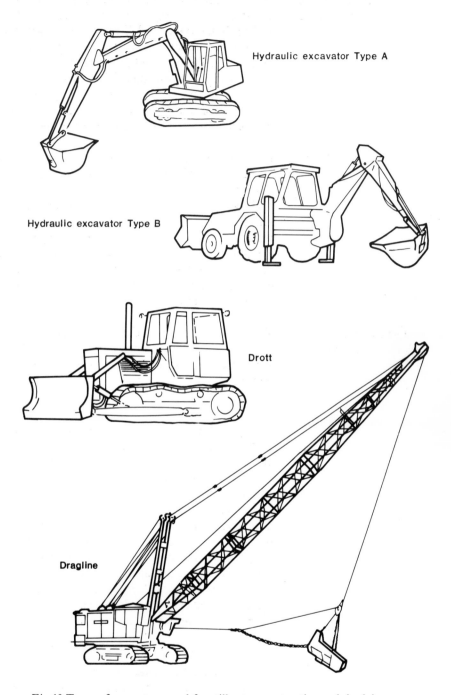

Hydraulic excavator Type A

Hydraulic excavator Type B

Drott

Dragline

Fig 40 Types of excavators used for stillwater construction and dredging operations

Drott

A drott can only be used when access to the pond bottom is possible, and where there is a solid base to the pond under the silt. Drotts can move the spoil and lift and dump it. They are generally used for landscaping work around pools.

Bulldozer

A bulldozer can only push soil, and requires access to the pond bottom which should therefore be firm under the silt. This type of machine can quickly move a large amount of spoil, and can be fitted with swamp tracks to prevent it sinking into silt.

Small punt-mounted excavator

This has a minimal reach and it is difficult to dispose of the spoil efficiently on the banks since the boat has to make repeated trips to the shore. With this machine it is possible to work nearer to power lines than with a dragline, and it can often reach parts of the pool that other excavators cannot.

Mud cat

The mud cat (*Fig 41*) works by sucking up silt from the lake bed through flexible pipes, and discharging it to specially constructed reservoirs on land. Its main disadvantage is that it is extremely costly to bring to site and, because of its size, it requires good access. It pumps away a great deal of water as well as silt, and there must be sufficient space around the pool for the construction of settlement lagoons (which often take more than a year to dry out thoroughly and consolidate).

It is usually best to obtain a quotation for the total cost of the job rather than hire a machine on an hourly basis; this is because the driver in these circumstances will require supervision and instruction while working and this may not be practicable for most fishery managers.

2.5 Control of aquatic plants

Water-plants are found in almost all aquatic situations in Britain, and are an essential part of the biology of rivers and lakes. A simplified summary of the role of plants in a fishery is shown in *Figure 42*. Aquatic vegetation is important because it:

- Aerates water by the process of photosynthesis. Much of the oxygen produced is removed by respiration during the day by animals, and at night by both plants and animals. During very warm weather the respiratory demand for oxygen may be so great that it falls to a level critically low for fish.

- Acts as a shelter for animals. Larger plants provide a refuge for

74

Fig 41 A mud cat showing the floating silt discharge pipe

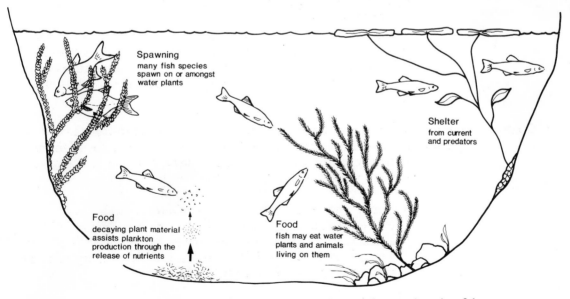

Spawning
many fish species
spawn on or amongst
water plants

Shelter
from current
and predators

Food
decaying plant material
assists plankton
production through the
release of nutrients

Food
fish may eat water
plants and animals
living on them

Fig 42 A diagram summarizing the role of water-plants in a fishery

animals, protect them from fast water currents, and hide them from predators. In addition, many species of fish and invertebrates deposit their eggs on plants. The presence of aquatic vegetation increases the productivity of a fishery, and a water that is rich in plant-life will generally contain more food for fish than one that possesses an impoverished flora. Too much vegetation can, however, lead to water quality problems and make angling difficult.

- Consolidates the bed and banks of a fishery. Plant roots help to bind the soil and prevent the banks from collapsing; rooted plants anchor gravel and stones, so making the bed more habitable for invertebrates, and vegetation absorbs the impact of current and waves and protects banks from erosion.

- Provides food for other organisms. Plants, whether living or dead, form a food source for many animals. Plant detritus, for example, is a major food item for many invertebrates, and aquatic vegetation is an important part of the diet of many cyprinid fish.

- Intercepts silt and plant debris. Plants reduce water velocity and raise water levels when they grow in running water. They may thus assist the deposition of silt and organic matter in some parts of the channel, and increase water velocity in other parts, thereby creating scour. In stillwaters, decomposing plant material can accumulate over the years. This increases the productivity of the pool, the density of growing plants, and helps to raise the bed, thus promoting the development of marshes and (ultimately) dry land.

Types of aquatic vegetation   Aquatic plants can be classified into four groups:

Emergent plants

These possess erect, aerial leaves arising from open water or mud. They grow where the water level is anything up to about half the maximum height of the plant.

Long narrow-leaved plants like grasses are called reeds; they include common reed, bur-reed, reedmaces, reed-grass and bulrush. Broad-leaved emergent plants include water plantain, arrowhead and great water dock.

Floating leaved plants

This group includes water lilies. Most of the plants are rooted in the bed and have long pliable stems, but a few, such as duckweed and frog-bit, drift on the water surface. Members of this group are often found growing together with emergent and submerged plants in water just over 1m deep. The free-floating species are found over virtually any water depth.

Submerged plants

These are commonly rooted in the mud, like Canadian pondweed and water milfoil, but a few are free-floating below the water surface, like ivy-leaved duckweed and hornwort. They are all completely submerged except at the flowering period when most extend their flowering shoots above the water (*eg* water milfoil and mare's tail).

Algae

Algae are primitive plants which are classified botanically according to the colour of pigment they contain. Filamentous green algae are common examples, often growing in entangled mats and known as 'blanket weed' or 'cott'. The group also includes many microscopic forms that float about in stillwater and give rise to dense 'blooms' when conditions are suitable for their rapid growth and multiplication.

Establishment and growth

Most troublesome plants are perennials: they die back in the winter and reproduce vegetatively each year from stems or rhizomes (underground runners). Some water milfoil produce turions, compact winter buds that drop to the bottom in the autumn and re-grow in the spring rather like seeds. Algae reproduce vegetatively from their own strands, or by producing spores.

Many of the perennial water plants re-grow very rapidly once growth has started in the spring. Water crowfoot, for example, begins growth in April or May and stems may reach lengths of 6m by the end of June. Re-growth after cutting in the summer is equally rapid if the plant is cut before it flowers, but is slower if cut after flowering.

Objective of control

It is clear from the foregoing that aquatic plants not only play an important role in the environment, but that they also have a variety of forms. Fisheries management should not aim to eradicate aquatic vegetation, but to control it, and this can be achieved in a number of ways.

Cutting

Cutting is one of the commonest methods of weed control, and operations usually start in May. In shallow rivers, plants can be trimmed by using hand scythes, but where this is not possible due to the depth of the water, chain scythes (*Fig 43*) may be used. Cutting at the wrong time of year can stimulate fast re-growth. Each plant has a different growth pattern, and more efficient and economic control can be achieved if cutting times are based on these growth patterns. Two operators are necessary to use a chain scythe; each man operates from his own bank, and the scythe is moved back and forth whilst

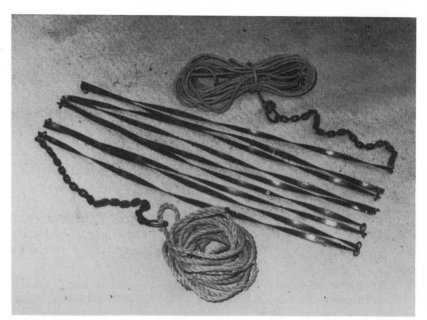

Fig 43 Chain scythes, or chain weed-cutters, may be used to cut water plants

moving upstream. A similar method can also be used on lakes. When cutting is carried out on a river, a stop-net should be used to prevent plants floating downstream and causing a nuisance to other water users. Cut plants must then be removed from the river. The weed cutting methods for a chalk stream, described by Richard Seymour, are shown in *Figure 44*.

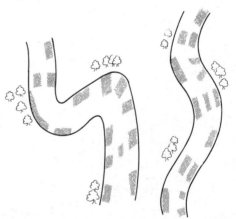

'Fishery Management and Keepering'.
Cutting river weed by the Side and Bar method.
– Proper cutting on bends can prevent lateral erosion of banks

Fig 44 Weed cutting in a chalk stream can control water flow and reduce bank erosion

78

For use on larger waters, a small, U-shaped mechanical cutter (*Fig 45*) is available for attachment to a dinghy. It has been introduced to Britain from the U S A and cuts a swathe about 1m wide to a depth of about 1m. The cutting blade is operated by a small engine mounted on the top of the knife frame. A rake attachment, which enables the boat to be used to collect the cut weed in standing water, is also available. It is also possible to purchase larger purpose-built weed-cutting boats, but these are expensive. Other means of cutting water weeds include excavator-mounted weed-cutting buckets for use on small watercourses.

Raking or 'cotting'

Rakes (*Fig 46*) are used to remove 'cott' from the water surface, and floating rope booms may be used to draw floating plants such as duckweed to the sides of a water where it can be removed. Rakes can also be employed to remove submerged aquatic plants like Canadian pondweed. Raking is a slow and labour-intensive technique, and is only really suited to small fisheries.

Fig 45 Specially designed weed-cutting boats can be used to control weed growth in larger watercourses

Fig 46 Rakes can be used to
remove floating weed

Ducks

Domestic ducks and other water-fowl that feed on water-plants can
be used to control plant growth in ponds by grazing. However, their
activities may also cause an increase in algal blooms.

Fish

Chinese grass carp (*Fig 47*) will consume large quantities of aquatic
plants in appropriate environmental conditions. Their rate of feeding
increases with rising water temperature: at temperatures below 16°C
their activities have very little effect, whereas food consumption is
greatest at about 25°C. At this temperature they can consume their
own weight in weed every day. It is probably unwise to stock with
grass carp less than 18–20cm long or 100g in weight because these

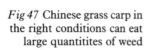

Fig 47 Chinese grass carp in
the right conditions can eat
large quantitites of weed

80

small fish are less efficient at eating plants. Brian Stott of the Ministry of Agriculture, Fisheries and Food has suggested that weed control in a pond could be achieved over a two-year period with a stocking rate of 200kg of grass carp per hectare, assuming summer water temperatures exceed 16°C for prolonged periods. (Such ideal conditions are rarely achieved in Britain.)

Grass carp are selective feeders, preferring the 'soft' plants such as stonewort and Canadian pondweed to the more fibrous ones such as water lilies and emergent water plants. Consequently, in some circumstances they may not control the unwanted plants, but instead overgraze those that are needed. It should not be forgotten that a pond that was initially stocked with the correct weight of grass carp may soon become overstocked as the fish grow. The subsequent loss of most or all of the valuable plant species may have a significant and long-lasting effect on the pond ecology. To effect controlled removal of excess weed, it may be necessary to remove some of these fish.

Efficient control may be possible if grass carp are used in conjunction with one of the more orthodox methods of control. It should be noted that there are legal restrictions on the introduction of grass carp into waters, details of which can be obtained from the Water Authorities.

If introduced into a pond in the correct density, carp will uproot the softer-stemmed plants whilst feeding in the pond mud. The increased turbidity that they create may exclude light and thus restrict or control plant growth.

Fertilization

The development of planktonic algal blooms which reduce light to a level that prevents the growth of rooted water plants has been used with success in America and in the British Isles. The pool is fertilized with soluble phosphate (eg 100kg triple super phosphate per hectare) in the early spring as the rooted vegetation begins to develop. Until the correct balance is achieved, unwanted filamentous algae may sometimes develop before the macrophytes develop fully.

Trees

Trees overhanging a water (Fig 48) can reduce light and so reduce aquatic plant growth. This shading effect is particularly noticeable beneath trees planted on the southern banks of rivers and lakes.

Polythene sheeting

It is also possible to create localized weed-free fishing areas in ponds by sinking weighted black polythene sheeting. This may be left in situ, or removed prior to fishing.

Herbicides

There are several different types of herbicide available for use in

Fig 48 Trees lining, and shading, a watercourse can reduce aquatic plant growth

water, and they have several distinct modes of action. Herbicides that kill the parts of the plant with which they come into contact are called contact herbicides. Herbicides that do not kill the plant rapidly in this way, but enter the plant itself, are known as translocated herbicides. As a general rule, only this latter group are any use in controlling re-growth of perennial water-plants. Herbicides can be further divided into non-selective types which will kill all plants, and selective forms which kill only certain species.

Before using any type of herbicide, it is important to identify the target plants on which they are to act. Accurate calculations must be made of the volume of water to be treated, using accurate data on water depth and area. Herbicides can be persistent and may prevent plant re-growth for many years, so great care must be exercised to prevent the unintentional death of all the aquatic plants present. If total eradication of plants takes place, the first species to recolonize are often the most undesirable in a fishery, like duckweed and filamentous green algae.

Small areas of the pond should be treated at a time. The main danger to fish life is not the toxicity of the herbicide, but the deoxygenation of the water following the death of the plants and their subsequent decomposition. Applications should be made before the plants are fully established since there will then be less vegetation to rot down; late spring is often an ideal period. On no account should a heavily weeded pond be overtreated in mid-summer as it is in these circumstances that fish are at greatest risk from deoxygenation.

Since an aquatic herbicide is defined as a pollutant, consent for its use must be obtained from the Water Authority. Herbicides can be extremely toxic to humans and cattle, and great care should be exercised during their use.

2.6 Habitat improvement in still and running waters

The fish species present in still and running waters are influenced by natural migration, transfer by animals, or transfers by man (both deliberate and accidental). The number of fish present and their size are determined by the physical, biological and chemical conditions of the fishery.

Carp, for instance, might grow to a large size, and breed successfully, in a shallow lowland pool that would not support brown trout. A large deep upland reservoir, on the other hand, may produce large trout but only a few small carp. Whilst it is important to stock waters with the species that are capable of flourishing in them, it is also possible to alter or improve the habitat to create better conditions for the fish. Habitat improvement methods are not recent innovations, but have been neglected recently in favour of that much over-used management technique – stocking (often overstocking). Habitat improvement, correctly applied, may well provide such excellent conditions for fish that destocking is necessary, and the removal and possible subsequent sale of these excess fish may provide sufficient money to fund further improvements. Although some of the available methods can be applied to both still and running water, these different habitats normally require separate techniques.

Physical improvement of stillwaters

The improvement of the physical habitat of stillwaters has received much attention in the U S A and is gaining popularity in European fisheries. It is particularly suitable in large deep waters that lack underwater features, because physical improvements provide sanctuaries of cover and shelter, spawning sites and areas of improved fish food production.

Brushwood reefs can be made by tying bushes together and weighting them so that they sink. More recently, reefs of old car and lorry tyres have been used effectively for the same purpose. These are inert, do not rust or corrode, and will not contaminate the water. It is suggested that these reefs should occupy no more than 0·25% of the total area of the lake, and that they be split into several separate units.

Old tyres are often available from garages at no cost – providing

83

they are collected. Each tyre will require several 2·5cm holes drilled in the upper tread to allow air to escape, and sufficient bricks wedged in place on the lower side to sink it. Reef designs are a matter of individual preference, but some are shown in *Figure 49*. Polypropylene or nylon cord or rope is used to lash the structures together, and the whole unit is lowered into position from a boat. These reefs require little or no maintenance.

2 Double Units

Triple Unit

Fig 49 Simple tyre reef designs, used as fish 'attractants' on the bottom of featureless ponds

Stacked Multiple Unit

Chemical improvement of stillwaters

The chemical nature of the water in a fishery is important as it often determines the biological productivity of that water. Acid water is normally less productive than alkaline water. It lacks certain essential chemical constituents and, in particular, is poorly supplied with calcium carbonate. These chemicals are essential for the healthy growth of many plants, and acid waters rarely support dense populations of the aquatic creatures that form the principal food of fish. Most coarse fisheries are at their most productive when they are slightly alkaline, with a pH of between 7·5 and 8·5.

It is possible to improve chemical conditions in new pools, and to reinstate the productivity of old pools, by various means that fall under the general heading of fertilization. Old established pools

84

decline in productivity with time because the nutrients necessary for plant growth become trapped deep in the pond mud. The pond soil turns increasingly acid, and the breakdown of organic matter like plants and leaves becomes slower. Fewer salts are released into the water because they become adsorbed onto colloids in acid conditions and, although they are present in the pond soil, they are not available to plants.

In order to increase the productivity of an established pool, it is often necessary to raise the pH or alkalinity of the pond mud to promote plant growth. This is generally carried out by using lime. Lime as calcium bicarbonate is also important since it provides reserves of the gas carbon dioxide which is necessary for the photosynthesis of green plants. New pools created in rich soil are normally quite productive, but pools such as gravel pits, clay pits, and sand pits are often nutrient-poor. In this situation, nutrients such as calcium need to be added, and these help to promote the formation of organically-based bottom sediments which consolidate the fine silt bed. Other nutrients important for plant growth (such as phosphates) may be in limited supply.

Fertilizers which can be used include hydrated lime which produces an alkaline reaction in the pond soil and aids the release of nutrients for uptake by plants. Lime should be spread over the pond bottom or water surface at a rate of 200–750kg/ha, and should be used in waters where there is a rich mud bottom. If fish are present in the pool, care should be taken to treat only a portion of the water surface and apply the lime at weekly intervals. Crushed limestone should be added to nutrient-poor ponds where there is little pond mud and a lack of calcium. The dosage rate is approximately 750–1 000kg/ha. Basic slag is a slow-release inorganic phosphate fertilizer that promotes plant growth. It should be added in the winter, when a dosage rate of 300kg/ha is normally recommended. Triple super phosphate is a soluble phosphate compound that quickly encourages algal blooms, which are in turn fed on by copepods and other crustacea. Although it may be expensive, it need only be applied at about 100kg/ha.

Note that the timing of fertilizer addition is often important. Hydrated lime and crushed limestone should be added in the winter. Limestone can be added together with basic slag, but hydrated lime and triple super phosphate should not be added together since they react to form an insoluble compound.

Other fertilizers include well rotted farmyard manure, which can be added at a rate of about 1kg/m². Great care must be used since the decomposition of organic manures in water can cause extremely low oxygen levels which may kill fish. Sewage sludges may also be used, but the same deoxygenation effects apply. If these are used, care must be taken to ensure that they do not contain toxic substances. If it is practical, dewatering a pool so that the pond mud dries out over winter will enrich it, since the pond mud will become oxidised in contact with air. When the lake is refilled, there will be a release of nutrient salts to the water, which will increase productivity.

Occasionally, enclosed and running waters may contain excess nutrients, and this eutrophication may promote excessive plant growth, thereby lowering summer dissolved oxygen levels, especially at night. The alleviation of the problem is best achieved by reducing the nutrient inflow, but dredging or rendering the nutrients inactive by chemical means can also be successful.

Biological improvement of stillwaters
The provision of reefs to increase fish numbers, and the fertilization of stillwaters to feed them, may produce a measurable improvement in the size and abundance of the fish present. It is also possible to assist this habitat improvement process by the deliberate addition of freshwater plants and animals.

It must be emphasized that although many 'stockings' of plants, fish food or fish are successful, many more are not. If the chemical and physical properties of the water do not suit a particular species, it will become extinct from the fishery sooner or later. Freshwater shrimps or snails, for example, will not survive in soft water.

Plant material and availability

Figure 50 shows a cross-section of a pond showing the different zones occupied by plants. The structure can be applied to rivers or lakes.

Generally, the vegetative parts rather than the seeds of plants are used for stocking. The roots or rhizomes can be purchased from a commercial nursery or aquarium, or transplanted from the wild. It must be pointed out that it is an offence to uproot any wild plant without the permission of the landowners, and in some cases even with permission (Wildlife and Countryside Act 1981). It may be possible to obtain stock plants from a nearby lake or pond, but in no circumstances should rare species of plants be dug up without the owner's permission. Where possible, only locally obtained or common plants should be used. The local County Naturalists' Trust or the Botanical Society of the British Isles will offer advice on the wisdom of using a particular species or about its rarity value.

Suitable plants (from Birch, 1964)

For the water's edge, watercress can be established by pushing cuttings into mud and anchoring them with stones. Marginal reeds and rushes may be planted in a similar manner.

For water up to 0·5m deep, water starwort, water milfoil and water buttercup are suitable.

For water 0·5–1·25m deep, broad-leaved pond weed and lilies of various types are suitable. The establishment of lilies will be accelerated if they are planted in sacks or cardboard tubs of 50:50 rotted manure and soil.

86

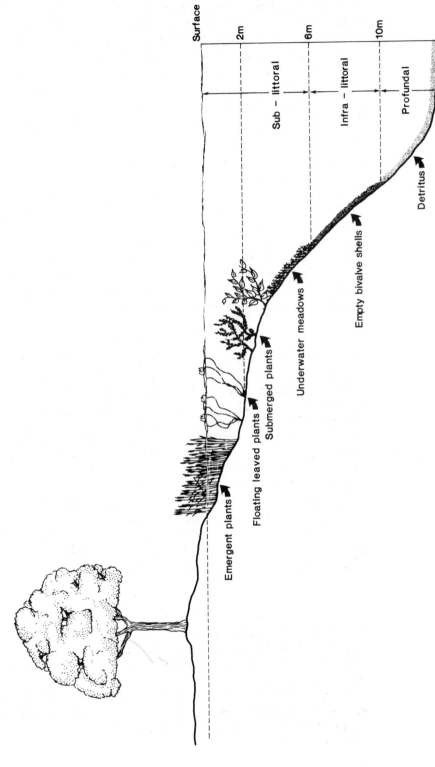

Fig 50 Cross section of a pond showing the different plant zones

For deeper water, stonewort is an excellent choice. There are, however, several plants to be avoided, like Canadian pondweed which can quickly choke a pool, and amphibious bistort for which there is no effective chemical control.

Planting

Submerged and floating leafed plants are generally planted by attaching a weight to the rhizomes and throwing them or dropping them into the water at the required place. In cases where there is very little organic matter on the bed of the lake, as with newly constructed lakes, it is advisable to put the rhizomes in a bio-degradable container, such as a sack containing soil and compost. Emergent species should be notch-planted in the shallow margins.

Animals

The most valuable introductions are often snails, pea and swan mussels, and freshwater shrimps. Shrimps should be released in shallow, hard water where the bottom is sandy and there are water-plant beds; snails are best 'sown' in shallow water where the bottom consists of stones.

Habitat improvement in running waters

Habitat improvement techniques in running water are confined to those of a physical nature; chemicals are quickly flushed out of a river (besides being illegal – in Britain – without the Water Authority's consent), and plants and animals can migrate if conditions are not suitable.

'Instream' river improvement devices include those that impound or modify river flow (current deflectors, low dams and weirs, bank stabilization devices *etc*); devices that provide direct cover (submerged shelters, artificial bank cover devices); and those that improve spawning areas.

Current deflectors (gabions, groynes and wing deflectors)

These structures utilize the natural river flow to create pools and riffles, increase water speed, and direct water flow. Some examples are shown on *Figure 51*.

Low dams

Low dams or weirs (*Fig 52*) are the most commonly used river improvement devices. Dams raise the water level above them and may provide more shelter for fish; after a while siltation may occur to such an extent that the original benefit of shelter is lost, but until this happens the settlement of silt behind small dams improves water quality. Below them, the water depth is reduced, and water speed increases, with scour holes forming. Bank erosion can be prevented by using one of the techniques discussed below.

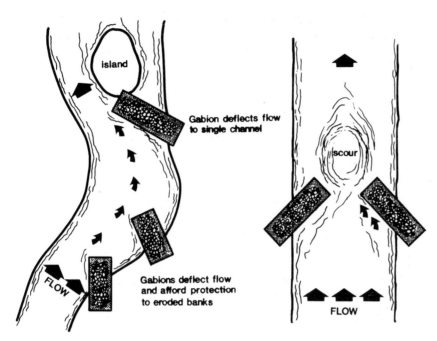

Fig 51 Some examples of current deflectors used in rivers to direct water flow for control of erosion

Gabion deflects flow to single channel

Gabions deflect flow and afford protection to eroded banks

Gabions sited to direct flow and result in the formation of a pool through scouring of the stream bed in shallow riffle areas of river

Gabions wire baskets filled with stone, may be sited to counter or deliberately create erosion of a rivers banks or bed.

Fig 52 This low weir on the River Penk, Staffs, has raised the upstream water level

Low dams are effective in recreating the pool and riffle nature of a stream. Typically, riffles occur at distances of between 5 to 7 channel widths, apart, down the stream. Where this natural pattern has been destroyed (perhaps by a land drainage scheme), it may be wise to incorporate deflector and dams at intervals of this length, the exact spacing depending upon the gradient of the stream.

Bank stabilization devices

Many factors may increase the erosion of banks, and this is often a significant contributor to an increased sediment load in rivers. Bank stabilisation techniques include stoning (*Fig 53*), piling and the fencing of areas likely to be affected by cattle or sheep.

Devices that provide direct cover

Shelter is important in order to provide cover for prey and predator; it also increases habitat diversity and provides spawning areas and

Fig 53 Bank erosion on this section of the River Trent has been stabilized by stoning

shading. Cover may encourage the colonization of invertebrates, and help fish to establish and recognize their territory.

Artificial cover devices

These are designed to serve the same function as overhanging banks, hedges or bank vegetation. The devices consist of platforms constructed above the water surface and held in position by piles driven into the bed (*Fig 54*). Floating overhanging platforms are an alternative solution.

Submerged shelters

Submerged shelters include branches, bushes or logs anchored to the river-bed, or submerged boulders or rocks. Such devices should provide minimum resistance to flow and should be designed to minimize the risk of trapping debris; for example, they should be placed in line with the flow, not across it.

Spawning area improvements

Most salmonid species, and some cyprinids such as dace and chub, spawn on gravel where the substrate size and the water speed and depth are suitable. It is possible to provide areas of gravel for spawning, but this is normally very costly. Gravel beds can also be raked over every year to remove silt. It is more feasible to use some of the previously mentioned devices (such as deflectors and dams) to create local eroding conditions to remove silt, so exposing suitable gravel deposits. It should be stressed that these devices should never be built without prior consultation with the local Water Authority.

2.7 Bankside vegetation

Trees are an essential part of the environment and are hosts to a large number of organisms – lichens, fungi, worms, liverworts, insects and other invertebrates, as well as mammals and birds.

Advantages and disadvantages of trees

Trees provide windbreaks, create cover for fish, and their small feathery roots are often used as a substrate for spawning. These roots may also provide cover for fish, while the abundant insect life which develops in the tree canopy augments the pond and river food supplies. The shade created by trees can also reduce weed development in pools and rivers. They have a valuable function in stabilizing the banks, preventing erosion of meandering river courses. Generally, the planting of trees on the bank of an otherwise barren watercourse will improve the fish-holding capacity of that water.

On the other hand, too many dead leaves settling and covering the bottom of lakes and ponds can smother underwater plants. Again, once they reach full height, trees bordering rivers create so much shade that no weed grows beneath them, the current is then drawn to the weedless area and bank erosion follows (*Fig 55*). They can also fall down, creating drainage problems (*Fig 56*).

(a) Section through platform

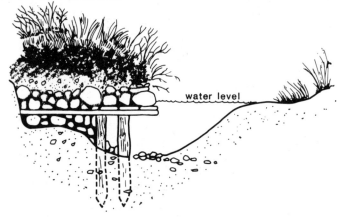

water level

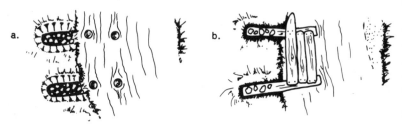

Fig 54 This diagram shows how a stream can be improved by constructing an emergent platform

(b) Stages of construction

a.

b.

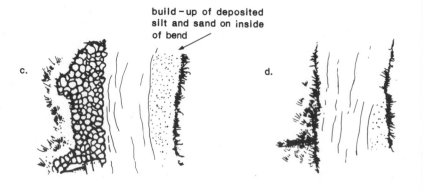

build-up of deposited silt and sand on inside of bend

c.

d.

Fig 55 Bank erosion can be caused by water being drawn to the weedless area created by excessive tree shade

Fig 56 Fallen trees can obstruct the free flow of water in a watercourse

93

Planting   Detailed guidance on how to plant and take care of trees is available
from many sources. A good guide is contained in the Forestry
Commission's leaflet *Trees and People*. Further advice is available
from the Nature Conservancy Council, Forestry Commission,
County Nature Conservation Trust and the Ministry of Agriculture,
Fisheries and Food.

It is preferable to plant trees in clumps rather than at uniform
intervals; apart from the aesthetic appearance, this allows access for
anglers. It may be possible in certain circumstances to receive a grant
for tree planting – *see Appendix 4*.

Types of tree suitable for   There are two main groups of trees that occur on the waterside: the
the waterside   alder and the willow families. Some trees like oak and ash prefer drier
habitats, but sometimes grow on the waterside as isolated trees or in
woods. If any removal of trees from the waterside is envisaged the less
easily managed species, like oaks, should be retained. The manage-
able trees are treated in different ways.

Alder and birch

Alder is probably the most common waterside tree. From the
fisheries aspect it ranks highly for the number of insects that inhabit
its foliage and ultimately fall in the water, thus acting as a food source
for fish. It can also be cut to the ground and allowed to shoot again
(*Fig 57*). New alders (plants about 1m in height) should be protected
from browsing animals for about ten years, by which time the leading
shoots will be well out of reach and the bark not easily damaged.
Silver birch is often planted, but the hairy birch is preferable as it
grows better in wet soils.

Willows

These are best managed by pollarding (*Fig 58*). The trees are cut
back at about 2·5–3·0m above ground and the new shoots grow from
the tip, out of reach of cattle. Willow trees are easy to establish if
straight branches are cut and rammed firmly into the ground at the
water's edge. Their shoots will require trimming every ten years or
so, providing material for other uses. The white willow and crack
willow will both provide good pollards. Smaller bush willows can be
propagated by cuttings. They should be cut back close to the ground
if they grow too large, and this action will also promote bush growth.

2.8 Control of pests   The aquatic world provides an attractive environment for many
and predators   different types of animal, with a vast range of habitats under, on or
near the water. A fisheries manager, in planning the development of
a particular fishery, should have decided on his plan of operation at
an early stage. This plan will give details of the species to be
encouraged at that water. He will also know from the plan which

94

Fig 57 Alders cut to the ground (pollarded)

other species of fish – or other animal – will be unwanted – a pest to his site or a predator on his stock.

A predator on one fishery may be the preserved and preferred specimen in another; pike, for example, may be unwanted on a specialist trout fishery, but preserved on a specimen pike fishery. It is therefore not possible to give an exact and definitive list of pests and predators. Essentially, there are three main types of animal (four if invertebrates are included) that fisheries managers may want to control: birds, mammals and fishes. There are many instances where it makes more sense to manage predators and 'pests' as part of the fishery, rather than to go to the effort of undertaking expensive and time-consuming control measures.

Problems caused by predators

There are four main problems that may arise on a fishery due to the presence of pests and/or predators:

95

Fig 58 Pollarded willows

- There can be direct predation on the preferred species, either by the predator eating or damaging stock.
- Disease and parasites can be spread by some species of animal.
- In many cases, physical damage is caused to banks.
- If the 'unwanted' species is present in excessive numbers, there can be an alteration of water quality.

Before undertaking control measures, fishery managers should remember the value of predators to fish stocks and man. They can remove fish weakened by disease and parasites, they can remove other predators, and they can control stunted fish populations. Predation on young fish by older fish of the same species is also normally high.

Birds   There are over 200 species of bird that live on or by the water. The vast majority are either better suited to marsh or estuary, or are visitors making use of a temporary food source.

The species that depend on water include representatives from several families. Those that feed on aquatic plants and animals often remain throughout the year, but the insectivores have to migrate when summer food supplies are not available. The ability of birds to react rapidly in adversity (they fly away!) gives them a clear advantage over other animals and makes them early indicators when anything disrupts lower levels of the food-chain. Climatic changes, increases in pollution, or subtle variations in amenity use can affect birds in spectacular ways, yet their adaptability enables them to cope with all but the most serious problems.

Heron

This is an unmistakable bird of the waterside, although it nests some distance away in tall trees. Though the heron has a widespread distribution in Britain, it is relatively scarce: the breeding population in England and Wales in 1979 was 5 400 pairs. The heron is carnivorous and captures small fish, tadpoles, frogs, small mammals, small birds, reptiles, molluscs and insects from shallow water. Peak feeding times are at dawn and dusk.

The daily food requirement of an adult heron is approximately 370g, but when young are being fed this figure is approximately doubled. In any natural fishery this supply of food is readily available, and control measures are rarely necessary. However, losses on trout farms can be significant. Calculations on one particular farm showed that during the peak feeding period between April and August, 1 818kg of trout were eaten by herons. When losses reach this level, fish farmers should take active steps to deter the birds.

Caging the site (Fig 59) is the complete answer, but the cost of this would be great on large farms. The effect of scaring devices such as scarecrows, gunfire and flashing lights last for only four or five days as the birds gradually get used to them. Other ways of reducing the fishing success of herons at fish farm pools are shown in Figure 60.

A dog trained to chase herons away is also a useful, if unusual, control method. If all else fails, there is provision in the Wildlife and Countryside Act 1981 (WLCA 1981) for an authorized person to kill herons with a legal method if it can be shown that such action is necessary for the purpose of preventing serious damage to the fishery.

Gulls

Under this heading come such species as the herring gull, black-headed gull, lesser black-backed gull and greater black-backed gull. It is now fairly well established that all such birds can spend a large part of their lives away from the sea. All species will eat almost anything edible, from fish to carrion and gleanings on rubbish tips.

97

Fig 59 Overhead wires to keep predatory birds away from ponds in a fish farm

The larger gulls will also take small birds, chicks, eggs *etc*. They will, given the opportunity, prey directly on fish, favouring the sort of easy prey that is available on trout farms. They are an important link in the life-cycle of eye fluke and for this reason alone should be actively discouraged. Trout farms in Denmark are required by law to place wires over their ponds to keep these birds away. Any of the methods used to control herons can also be employed.

In Britain there is provision in the WLCA 1981 to kill herring, lesser black-backed and greater black-backed gulls by authorized persons; though it should be remembered that certain gull species are Schedule 1 protected birds.

Cormorants

The cormorant is common in coastal waters, but can also live on inland lakes and reservoirs. Most colonies are on rocky seashore inlets and ledges, whereas inland they usually nest in trees which eventually die as a result of the guano deposits. Cormorants rarely visit fish farms as they require bigger expanses of water. However, they do visit waters in the Midlands of England whilst on passage. In Britain there is provision in the WLCA 1981 for an authorized person to kill cormorants with a legal method to prevent damage to a fishery.

Ducks

Some species of duck such as tufted duck are thought to prey on small fish. This duck dives to depths of 2–3m for its food – normally crustaceans, molluscs, insects and their larvae, as well as vegetable matter. If ducks are allowed to congregate in numbers on small pools,

a) Earth banks gradient $<60^{\circ}$

FISHING EASY

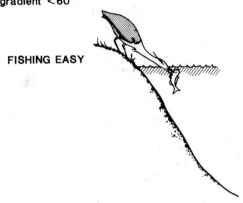

Fig 60 Other ways of reducing the success of herons at fish farm pools

b) Twine and floats

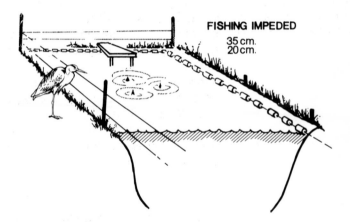

FISHING IMPEDED
35 cm.
20 cm.

c) Reinforced banks
Low water level

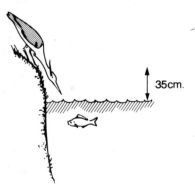

35cm.

their droppings can affect the water quality. There is also a risk of passing on parasites to the fish in the water. Ducks can be controlled by most of the methods employed to discourage herons. In Britain there is provision in the WLCA 1981 to kill certain species in the open season from August to February.

Grebes

The great crested grebe and lesser grebe or dabchick feed their young on small insects, molluscs *etc*. The diet of the adult bird consists mainly of fish and insect larvae. Grebes very rarely visit the ponds on fish farms, and appear to prefer lakes and gravel pits. There are no records of control operations against this species, and it is not lawful to kill them.

Kingfisher

This bird nests in a burrow excavated in a steep bank or embankment, and a pair of birds can have two clutches between April–July, each of six to seven eggs. The kingfisher catches small fish up to 10cm long, and also crustaceans and water insects. When hunting prey it dives into the water from a bankside perch. If the owner wants to discourage these birds on fish farms containing fry, the ponds should be covered with fine mesh. In Britain, kingfishers are protected by special penalties under Schedule 1 of the WLCA 1981.

Other birds

Many birds have been observed taking fry from fish pens, tanks and ponds, probably because the fry are easy to catch. They include moorhens, coots, blackbirds, crows, robins and wagtails. All that is needed to discourage them is to cover the tanks with netting or wire mesh.

Mammals Mammals that are semi-aquatic and adapted to live near or on water usually have good fur. In addition, species like the otter are adapted to aquatic life with webbing between their toes and a strong muscular tail. The fisheries manager will also come across other mammals, such as the brown rat and mole which frequent the land near water.

Water vole

Water voles are territorial: males have territories of about 130m^2 while females take up smaller areas. They restrict themselves for most of the time to the edges of waters, and make tunnels in the banks with exits above and below water level. They feed on the leaves, stems and roots of waterside plants such as reeds and grasses.

The main problem associated with this animal is that its burrows can lead to serious bank erosion. Cages baited with fresh apple, lettuce or carrots will catch them alive, after which they can be transported and released elsewhere. Total eradication is very difficult, but may be achieved by offering poisoned grain at bait stations.

Otter

Otters are now rare in all areas and absent from most. They are essentially animals of rivers and marshes. Male otters may travel up to 10km per night in search of food – usually fish or other aquatic life. A male otter is longer than a fox (about 120cm) and twice its weight: mink, which can be wrongly identified as otters, are only half this size, at 60cm. In Britain, otters are fully protected under the WLCA 1981.

Mink

This animal originated in North America, and in Britain is bred in captivity for its fur pelt. The first record of escapees breeding successfully in Britain was in 1956, and mink have now spread to many areas. They are very efficient nocturnal predators, killing fish, moorhens and voles.

The animal can be killed legally, and MAFF offer advice on their control. The Mink and Coypu (Keeping) Order, in effect up to 1987, prohibits the keeping of these two animals in Great Britain except under licence. The legislation also requires occupiers who know of any unlicensed mink or coypu on their land to inform the appropriate agricultural department.

Coypu

The coypu has become established in East Anglia (mainly in Norfolk, Suffolk and North Essex) following escapes from coypu farms in the 1930s and 1940s. Adult coypus are easily recognized by their large size; males reach an average of nearly 7kg and are almost 1m long from nose to tail–tip. They are almost entirely vegetarian but will eat freshwater mussels. Their burrows are about 20cm in diameter with a half-submerged entrance, and they penetrate for several metres away from the water, thus lowering the strength of flood banks.

A scheme to eradicate wild coypu was launched in 1981 by the Anglian Water Authority and Internal Drainage Boards. The animals are caught alive in cage traps and then killed humanely.

Mole

This animal feeds almost exclusively on worms, and builds complex tunnel systems on different levels. The mounds thrown up along the tunnels may interfere with fishery bank maintenance operations such as grass cutting. In extreme cases it is possible that the tunnels may weaken banks.

Common rat (brown rat)

The common, or brown, rat is widely distributed, and can carry fish

101

diseases as well as diseases that affect man. It is a very adaptable animal and, if it lives beside water, soon becomes expert at diving and swimming beneath the surface. Its burrows are generally dug in banks or other raised ground, and are complicated branching systems with nest chambers at intervals. They sometimes extend for several metres at a depth up to 50 cm.

Breeding takes place at all times of the year with up to 16 young born at a time. Young rats are easy prey for predators such as owls, foxes, stoats, weasels and cats, and both foxes and cats will take full-grown rats.

Rats can be a major pest on a fish farm, for example, by fouling and damaging fish food bags, and damaging nets and ropes. The animals can be trapped, poisoned, or hunted with ferrets or dogs. Probably the most effective way to control, if not eradicate this pest, is to carry out a properly designed poisoning programme. However, it is better to prevent rat problems by proper management than to have to resort to poisoning. Proofing buildings against rats, although more expensive, is a far better method of control.

Fish Unwanted fish stocks can be removed by any of the methods described in Section 1.6.

Invertebrates Some of the more serious predators at hatcheries can be invertebrates such as water beetles, dragonfly nymphs, water boatmen and water bugs. Some of these may cause enormous losses to young fish if not controlled.

2.9 Protection of fish stocks by regulations

Most of the text so far has been devoted to establishing viable fisheries by paying attention to the various means that are available for their improvement. The other aspect is that of regulating the pressure on those stocks so as to ensure that as far as possible they are maintained to give the best possible sport.

Fishery managers are warned that this section is specifically written with the intention of pointing out the techniques available, and generally how to apply them. *It is not intended to be, nor should it in any sense be used as, guidance for legal purposes.*

Techniques available for this purpose include: close seasons; closed areas (or sanctuaries); a catch limit (or a bag limit); a gear limit; restrictions on the type of gear; size limits. All these methods are used in one form or another on fisheries in the British Isles (*Table 4*).

Close seasons Minimum close seasons are mandatory in England and Wales for all species but they may be removed by byelaw in the case of rainbow trout and the eel. They may also be modified by byelaws made by the Water Authority, but may not be reduced in length. Their usual purpose is to enable fish to spawn unhindered and to allow them to recover from the effects of spawning. Certain exceptions are allowed,

102

Table 4 SUMMARY OF REGULATORY METHODS AND THEIR EFFECTS

	Act of Parliament	Water Authority byelaws	Owner's rules	Main effects	Incidental effects
1. Close seasons	—	May modify or waive in case of eels or coarse fish	May be extended	To protect fish during breeding	Protects growing crops, nesting birds or, in winter, roosting waterfowl
2. Sanctuaries	—	Rarely	Occasionally	Restrict the catch of fish	As above
3. Bag limit	—	Occasionally		Eases pressure on stocks when conditions favour big catches	May be frustrating to anglers on such days
4. Gear limit	Occasionally on commercial methods only	Often	On numbers of permits/rods	Prevents overcrowding, reduces damage to stocks	Require a balance between quantity and quality
5. Type of gear	Generally restrict permissible methods to rod and line, or licensed nets *etc* for commercial fishery	Apply mainly to commercial methods	Fine tuning in line with objectives of fishery	Best sport	
6. Size limit	Except in the case of salmon	Occasionally	Can be tailored to the particular fishery	Assist in maintaining breeding stock and optimise quality of sport	

the more important of which are:

- For the purpose of artificial propagation of fish, or the stocking or restocking of waters, or for some scientific purpose, with the prior permission, in writing, of the Water Authority.
- Eels, freshwater fish or rainbow trout removed by the owner or occupier of a fishery where salmon and trout are specially preserved.
- Fishing with rod and line in any such fishery with the permission in writing of its owner or occupier.
- Fishing for eels where such fishing is authorized by a byelaw.
- Fishing for coarse fish or rainbow trout for scientific purposes.
- Taking coarse fish for bait with the permission in writing of the owner.

Sanctuaries   These are areas within a fishery where angling is not allowed. They are useful and effective, particularly in fisheries where trout, for example, are removed: they greatly slow down the impact of angling on the stock of fish and are therefore very effective in evening out the short-duration surge in catches that follows the introduction of stock fish. On enclosed waters even a large sanctuary area will not greatly reduce the numbers of trout that are eventually caught during the course of a season.

Bag limits   Bag limits are commonly applied on a per day or per visit basis to fish which are to be removed from the water. There is not usually a case for bag limits on fisheries where the catch is returned, although they could be considered in the case of specimen fisheries.

Gear limits   These restrict the number of rods that may be used on any particular water. In one form or another they are fairly common practice on smaller inland waters, particularly those controlled by clubs or syndicates developing specimen fisheries. They serve the dual purpose of regulating the amount of fishing that is taking place and, therefore, spreading out the pressure on the fish whether these are removed or not. They also reduce the chance of interference by, or crowding of, anglers themselves.

Type of gear   This chapter is principally concerned with fishing with rod and line, but within this description it is possible to stipulate the method in relation to the size of hook, breaking strain of line, and the technique – whether this involves the use of a float, a spinner or a fly, live bait, maggots, worms, *etc.* Within the limitation of rod and line angling, the restriction is really directed towards ensuring that the type of fishery that is being managed is in fact providing the sport for which it was designed. Within the much wider context, it is the main way in which the fisheries laws and byelaws safeguard the natural and augmented stocks of fish in inland waters from all the various possible techniques of removal. It is also important to pay attention to restrictions on type of gear in any fishery where the fish are to be removed and replaced, and to avoid the possible unwanted catching of, and resultant damage to, non-target species. In fisheries stocked with large trout, for instance, regulations may stipulate that the breaking strain of the line must exceed a certain number of pounds. The intention of this is to avoid breakages which result in trout escaping with the hook still embedded in their jaws.

Size limits Size limits are very often applied to fisheries where the target fish are removed as a matter of course. The object is to prevent the wasteful removal of fish that are not yet large enough to provide optimum sport, or that are not yet of a size at which they will breed. The size at which a fish species may breed is related to the environment in which it is growing. The calculation of the best size limit will be a matter for each fishery to decide. Like most of the techniques available, it does not offer complete control. If, for instance, all or nearly all the breeding stock are removed after they have had a chance to breed only once, then the size of eggs that will be laid will be at the smaller end of the natural range, since this often depends on the size of the female fish. This can in turn lead to reduced fry viability. In very heavily-fished water it may be advisable to impose a fairly large size limit to allow for this, whereas in waters that are only very lightly fished, a size limit becomes of much less importance.

Regulations Regulations in England and Wales are made at three different levels. The first is that of Central Government, as expressed in the Salmon and Freshwater Fisheries Act 1975 and in other similar legislation. The function of this Act is to provide a framework within which more local regulations may apply. The Act of Parliament is divided into sections: Section 1 prohibits the use of a number of instruments for catching fish, including snatches, spears, guns and set lines; Section 2 prohibits the taking of breeding fish, and the eggs of fish (which are sometimes used as bait by poachers); Section 3 regulates the use of nets; Section 4 prohibits the use of poisons, and creates the offence of releasing poisonous substances into waters containing fish; Section 5 prohibits the use of explosives, and regulates the use of electrical devices for catching fish; Sections 6–18 deal with obstructions· in watercourses that are frequented by migratory fish; Sections 19–24 deal with the close seasons and times at which fish may not be legally sold, *etc* and these are further elaborated in the Schedules to the Act. Schedule 1 deals with close seasons and times, and Schedule 3 specifies those matters which may be dealt with further by byelaw. These clearly relate to the techniques of regulation described above, and unless the particular section provides that they may be modified

105

or waived by byelaws made more locally by Water Authorities, then they apply to the whole country.

Byelaws are made by Water Authorities and are meant to take account of the more local conditions in their region. They may relate to the whole or part of that region, and to the whole or part of the year. They can thus be used flexibly in order to cater for local conditions and, in particular, for the various types of commercial fishery that exist around the shores of England and Wales. Although there is less need to vary them in the case of inland fisheries, certain local differences apply, and every fishery manager should be sure that he is equipped with a copy of the byelaws for his particular Water Authority. Water Authority byelaws quite commonly vary the close season for trout and sometimes that for coarse fish as well. They may or may not have the effect of making it lawful to fish for eels during the close season for freshwater fish. They also not infrequently include byelaws relating to fish that breed in their waters. Trout and grayling are almost always included, but coarse fish are not, because of the almost universal practice of returning them following capture. It is worth reflecting that, in the absence of such byelaws, there is no obligation upon an angler to return the coarse fish, and the fishery manager may well consider that there is a case for making some such rule for the waters under his control. It will be seen that byelaws usually have the effect of making the provisions of the Salmon and Freshwater Fisheries Act somewhat more restrictive than otherwise.

The third tier of regulation rests with the owner or occupier of the particular fishery. These 'rules' do not necessarily have the same legal powers as those inherent in byelaws and the sections of the Salmon and Freshwaters Fisheries Act, and they would not be enforced by officers of the Water Authority. The latter have a right of access under the Water Resources Act 1963 to cross land to enforce the provisions of the Salmon and Freshwater Fisheries Act and of their byelaws. The Theft Act 1968 in Schedule 1, however, makes it an offence for any person to fish in private waters other than with the consent of the owner or occupier of those waters. It has been successfully argued that any person fishing in these waters who is specifically in breach of any of the conditions under which he obtained his permission to do so, would have rendered that permission invalid and would, therefore, be breaking the law.

The fisheries manager will want to consider very carefully the exact results of his fishery management and may then have to decide whether or not he wishes to add anything to the provisions of the Act or the Water Authority byelaws. He may wish to make stipulations regarding the parking of vehicles, the routes by which the water may be approached, the use of portable radios, and so on. There is, sadly, a tendency for some owners to produce a list of several dozen such mini-rules and regulations.

106

Part 3: Exploitation

By this stage the fisheries manager will have a very clear idea of how the fishery should be used or exploited. This section explores the various ways in which this can be achieved, and also describes the different methods of aquaculture. Additionally, some indication is given of the needs of other recreational water users and how the business-minded fishery manager could use his fishery for other purposes.

3.1 Angling requirements and methods

In common with most recreational pursuits, the enjoyment that anglers derive from their sport is closely linked to quantifiable goals that they set themselves. These might include catching a particularly large fish of a certain species, winning an angling competition, or making a large catch of fish. It follows that the angler's basic need is for fish, be they large, numerous or of a certain species. There are, however, many other factors that contribute to making a fishing trip or a fishery enjoyable. Indeed, for some anglers a quiet picturesque fishery may be more important than the fish it contains.

General requirements

As most anglers travel to and from the fishery on a daily basis, it is important that car parking facilities and access to the water's edge are good. Obviously, a large clearly marked-out car park with a firm base is preferable to a section of marshy ground on which cars are haphazardly parked or, worse, become stuck. Secure litter bins, emptied regularly, will help to prevent the parking area becoming untidy.

Approved routes to the fishery should be clearly labelled, and anglers should be able to cross any obstructions such as hedges and streams easily and safely. If access routes are poor or inadequately signposted, there is risk of damage to crops or fences. The banks themselves should be safe, and there should be a well-defined path leading to the fishing areas. Signs should be firmly secured. If they are to be placed on trees or buildings, it is wise to fix them higher than 3m from the ground to help prevent them being removed or defaced by vandals.

Most fisheries are made more enjoyable if some measures are taken to provide firm, level and safe stations from which to fish. These may consist of simple, flat areas that have been cut into the bank, or of more elaborate platforms or fishing stages. If the fishery is popular or if angling competitions are held on it, it is worth numbering these fishing stations consecutively.

In Britain, angling is the most popular of all outdoor water sports (except perhaps for swimming) with participation estimated to be 3 380 000 in 1980. Of this total number of anglers 53% engaged in sea angling, 20% in game angling and 60% in coarse angling. Coarse or freshwater fishing can be further divided into pleasure angling and match angling. Many freshwater anglers take up the sport as a means of getting out into the open air, and the popularity of angling may be linked to its therapeutic value, or to the satisfaction that is gained by utilizing the hunting instinct which is said to lie in everyone. Whereas the pleasure angler pits his skills and wits against the fish, the match angler competes with other anglers by attempting to catch the heaviest weight of fish in a given time. The Water Space Amenity Commission identified the needs of coarse fishermen as follows:

'the basic, essential resource is an area of water well stocked with fish. The best conditions include a limited but varied bankside growth, some aquatic weed, and tree shade – particularly on the southern banks of rivers and streams. In well fished areas, a stretch of at least seven metres of bank for each angler is desirable. Strong or strengthened banks are required for safe access along rivers and streams, with occasional car parking facilities with toilets and refuse disposal facilities.'

Game fishermen require even more space and undisturbed water than other anglers. On rivers the ideal is a meandering channel with slow moving, deep areas, shallow riffles with a sandy or pebbly bed, cover for fish, and a wide variety of lighting conditions. Many British rivers and nearly all reservoirs are stocked to provide a supply of catchable-sized trout, although there are some natural self-sustaining populations. Salmon fisheries usually contain fish that are naturally bred, but a few rivers contain fish originating from eggs, fry or smolts stocked in preceding years.

Improvement of access facilities

There are several types of operation that a fisheries manager can undertake to improve access to a fishery. It is important, however, to check with the owner (if the fishery is leased), or with other interested parties (if the water is owned). Local neighbouring farmers, and persons controlling shooting rights, should be informed of any proposals that may affect their right of access.

Stiles

Properly constructed stiles prevent damage to fences, hedges and

108

gates (*Fig 61*). Single plank bridges (with supporting handrail), placed over small dykes will also prevent damage to the banks. The construction of a stile at one end of such a bridge will also control cattle.

Cattle grids

Normally, a farmer will install a grid in place of a gate where traffic volume would render the latter unacceptably inconvenient. In certain circumstances such as at the entrance to a busy car park (*Fig 62*) it may be worthwhile constructing one, but this operation should be undertaken or supervised by qualified engineers.

Fencing

Fences (*Fig 63*) to control the movement of cattle should be constructed whenever possible, and suitable material may be available from local pollarded trees. Cattle drinks should be lined with stone to control bank erosion, and fenced midway across the stream.

It is important to discuss the location and construction of fencing with the local farmer, and land drainage engineers of the Water Authority will also need to be consulted if the watercourse is

Fig 61 A simple stile on the main footpath helps to prevent damage to fences and hedges

109

Fig 62 A cattle grid to
control moorland livestock

Fig 63 Riverside fencing to
keep cattle from trampling
banks

maintained by the Authority. Drainage byelaws of some Water Authorites forbid anyone 'without the consent of the Authority to erect or place in the river any fence, stake, post, fishing rack, pen or enclosure for birds or fish'. It is always better to check first and so avoid the additional expense of removing the obstruction after it has been erected.

Angling platforms The types of angling platform that are acceptable by many Water Authority engineers are shown in *Figures 64* and *65*. Woods such as oak and elm (if available) may be utilized, and these should be treated to prevent premature rotting. Angling platforms should be constructed to allow water to drain back into the river, as the wood is likely to split and become unsafe if the platform retains water after floods.

Fig 64 Simple angling station constructed from concrete slabs

Permanent pegs Many angling organizations that have long leases and allow fishing competitions construct permanent 'pegs', (*Fig 66*) which mark designated fishing stations. These are often short, numbered concrete, metal or wooden stakes. Consent from the relevant drainage engineer (as well as from the farmers and riparian owner) is often required if the banking is mowed by the Water Authority, as fixed pegs can interfere with grass mowing. Alternatively, concrete slabs of about $0.25m^2$, can be inset into the banking: this enables grass cutting equipment to cut immediately over the 'peg', and provides a clean stable fishing area.

111

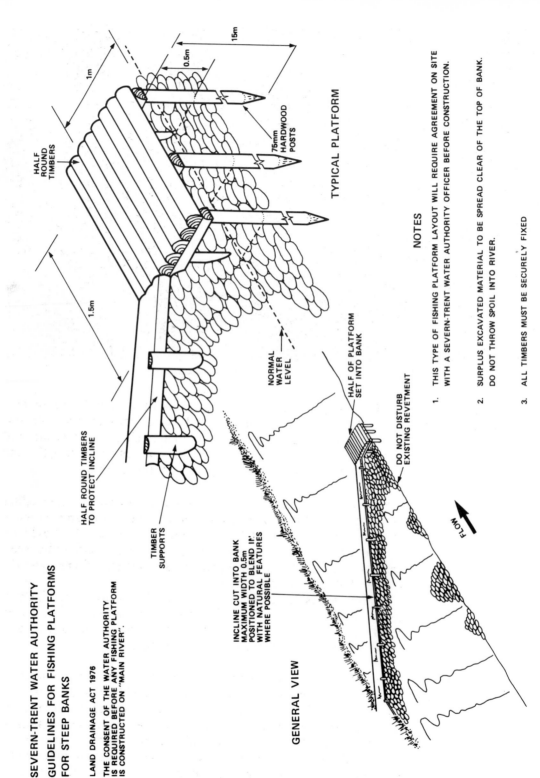

SEVERN-TRENT WATER AUTHORITY

GUIDELINES FOR FISHING PLATFORMS FOR STEEP BANKS

Land Drainage Act 1976

THE CONSENT OF THE WATER AUTHORITY IS REQUIRED BEFORE ANY FISHING PLATFORM IS CONSTRUCTED ON "MAIN RIVER".

HALF ROUND TIMBERS

HALF ROUND TIMBERS TO PROTECT INCLINE

TIMBER SUPPORTS

1m

1.5m

15m

0.5m

75mm HARDWOOD POSTS

NORMAL WATER LEVEL

TYPICAL PLATFORM

GENERAL VIEW

INCLINE CUT INTO BANK MAXIMUM WIDTH 0.5m POSITIONED TO BLEND IT WITH NATURAL FEATURES WHERE POSSIBLE

HALF OF PLATFORM SET INTO BANK

DO NOT DISTURB EXISTING REVETMENT

FLOW

NOTES

1. THIS TYPE OF FISHING PLATFORM LAYOUT WILL REQUIRE AGREEMENT ON SITE WITH A SEVERN-TRENT WATER AUTHORITY OFFICER BEFORE CONSTRUCTION.

2. SURPLUS EXCAVATED MATERIAL TO BE SPREAD CLEAR OF THE TOP OF BANK. DO NOT THROW SPOIL INTO RIVER.

3. ALL TIMBERS MUST BE SECURELY FIXED

Fig 65 Construction details of a timber angling platform

Fig 66 Anglers fishing from match-fishing pegs

3.2 Formation and management of angling clubs

It often happens that several anglers with a natural interest in a particular type of fishing or fishery decide to put their friendship on a more formal basis by forming an angling club. The formation of such a club can be of great benefit to all members – providing that the club is started correctly, with a good basic set of rules.

Objectives of the rules

There is nothing difficult in preparing the basic rules of an angling club, and a good starting point is to obtain a handbook from another angling club, or to read further about the subject. It should be remembered that rules are used to govern internal affairs between member and member; the appointment of various officers; and the aims and objectives of the club.

One of the first major decisions that members of a club are likely to make concerns the terms of its lease for a particular fishery, or negotiation for the purchase of one, and it would be sensible for any angling club to seek legal advice on this subject.

Management of angling clubs

A few of the larger angling associations employ full-time officers to look after their interests. These officials should be as familiar with commercial and financial matters as employees in any other business. The great majority of angling clubs, however, are run by honorary part-time officers, and the onus falls on them to familiarize themselves with all matters that are likely to affect the interests of the club, including any legislation that affects the club's interests. The

113

National Federation of Anglers (Appendix 3) will be able to offer advice to club officials on administrative matters.

Assessing the value of a fishery

Many of the factors affecting the value of a fishery are not obvious, and the angling club official is strongly advised to seek professional legal and financial advice before completing any deal to purchase or rent a fishery.

Angling organizations have few paid officials, and it is often only the club officials who claim for out-of-pocket expenses. It may be argued that in assessing the value of a fishery, those administrative charges that are often not claimed, *should* be included. Pegging fees, percentage profit on sale of day tickets, national taxes and local rates must all be considered as additional running costs. Some of the factors affecting the value of a fishery are shown on *Figure 67*.

In making an assessment it is important to gather as much information about the fishery as possible, and details of past fisheries survey work performed by the Water Authority is often available to the angling club wishing to lease or purchase that water. The price paid for adjoining fisheries, if this information is available, is sometimes the only guide to the true market value of the fishery. Angling clubs are, however, often very reluctant to advise non-members of their organization's financial affairs. In the last analysis, it is only the prospective buyer who knows how much he can afford, and how important it is to gain control of a particular stretch of water.

Lake fisheries

Purchase and rental

Generally, any person buying a fishery should expect to pay in excess

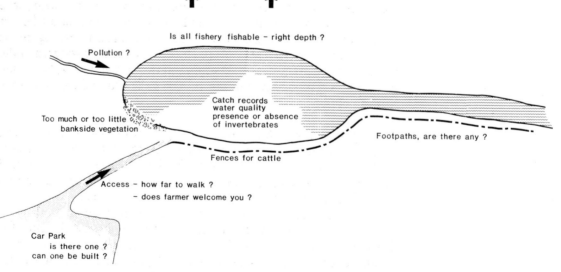

Fig 67 Diagram showing some of the main factors that affect the value of a fishery

114

of that charged for good agricultural land. A good coarse fishery can cost up to twice as much, whilst a 'put-and-take' trout fishery can cost much more, depending on its quality.

The rental value of a fishery often varies from one twelfth to one fifteenth of the purchase price. Gravel pits may be valued at less than this, but individual riparian owners sometimes tend to overprice their fisheries.

Assessment of potential income and running cost of day ticket trout fisheries

It is important for most buyers to be able to pay the annual running costs of a trout fishery from the income generated from it. The maximum income can be calculated once it is known how many anglers can fish the water at any one time, and the length of the fishing season. As a rule of thumb, each angler fishes 60m from another, thus providing sufficient space for safe and efficient casting. It is very unusual for the maximum number of anglers to visit a fishery every day of the season, and consequently it would be sensible to use a figure of less than 50% bankside occupancy from which to calculate the maximum possible income. Past records of income from waters, if available, should be treated only as a guide. They are often highly dependent on the frequency of stocking, the number and size of fish stocked, and the publicity given to the fishery.

The main running cost at a stocked trout fishery is the purchase of takeable trout, and this can make up 80% of total expenditure. Other items of expenditure include bailiff wages, rates, upkeep of bailiff's house, grass cutting, advertising, depreciation and bank charges.

Coarse fisheries

The maximum number of anglers able to fish a coarse fishing lake (*Fig 68*) is dictated by the shape and state of the banks, and whether or not the shallows are fishable. Maximum income can again be calculated from the number of anglers that can fish the water, and the length of the fishing season. Running costs will again vary, but a well balanced coarse fishery will not need regular expenditure on stock fish.

River fisheries The number of trout fishermen that can comfortably fish a river (and hence the potential income) is restricted by the nature of, and access to, the water. High banks, heavy bankside vegetation, trees and bushes, excessive weed growth and long walking distances are all major discouragements to an angler wanting to fly-fish.

A good coarse river fishery may command the same price as a trout fishery, but its value is influenced by the supply and demand for fisheries of the same type. The value of coarse fishing rivers near urban conurbations will obviously be higher than that of similar rivers far from cities or towns.

115

Fig 68 Anglers fishing from the banks of a lake

3.3 Commercial exploitation of coarse fish

Farming carp for food was a widespread practice until, at the end of the nineteenth century, marine fish became freely available in places distant from the sea. In recent years there has been a small but constant demand for carp, eels, bream, roach and a few other species for food, particularly in large towns with a European immigrant population.

Only a few of the anglers using rod and line retain coarse fish for food. Any of the methods described in Section 1.6 could be used to capture and remove them but because of low demand very few are employed. Several specialist types of gear have, however, evolved to catch elvers and eels.

Elvers

The European eel spawns in the Sargasso Sea in the southwest Atlantic. The larval eel (leptocephalus) is carried by water currents for three years, and then changes into an elver as it approaches the continental shelf. It then migrates up the western coast of Europe

116

from Portugal and is found in greatest numbers in the rivers flowing into the Bay of Biscay. Some elvers also enter the Mediterranean and are caught in Italy and Egypt. The seasons and size of elvers varies considerably: *see Table 5*.

Table 5 SEASONAL SIZE OF ELVERS IN DIFFERENT REGIONS

Country	Time of Year	No/kg
Portugal and Spain	December/January	2 700/kg
French Coast	February	2 800/kg
Britain, Denmark, Holland	April/May	3 500/kg
Egypt	January/February/March	4 500/kg

Most British rivers have an elver run, and the best known of these is on the River Severn. As the elvers enter the estuary they are transparent, and at this stage are called 'glass eels'. Here they undergo a number of behaviour changes and show maximum activity during darkness. They change again as they pass up river and become progressively more pigmented ('black elvers'). Active migration does not usually occur below 6°C. The largest surface migrations occur in conjunction with phases of the moon, thus coinciding with spring tides and producing a characteristic rhythmic 14-day pattern. Vast numbers of elvers enter the Severn and other rivers in each spring tide cycle between March and mid-May, and with each tide of the cycle the 'zone' of elvers moves progressively upstream. This zone of exploitation is between three and ten kilometres in length. As the flood tide passes up the river, the elvers appear to be randomly distributed within the zone, but as soon as the tide ebbs, the elvers respond to the flow of the river and become concentrated in a dense ribbon against each bank. It is at this time that they become vulnerable to fishermen using the traditional hand-held elver net (*Fig 69*). This is similar to a scoop, and is made of cheesecloth stretched tightly over a willow frame approximately 1m long, 0·5m wide and 0·5m deep. The net is dipped into the river and held there for a few minutes before being lifted and drained; the elvers being tipped into a bucket. They are then placed in flat muslin-based stacking trays, each holding 2kg, before being taken by the fishermen to one of the elver stations for sale, storage and distribution. Any debris and dead elvers are removed, and the live elvers are stored in recirculating systems (although prolonged storage leads to weight loss). Some elver stations specialize in producing deep-frozen elvers.

Elvers caught in recent years have gone to Spain as food; to other European countries for restocking; and occasionally to Japan for growing on in commercial eel farms. The market in the British Isles is now expanding and there is a demand for elvers for restocking and for growing on in eel farms which utilize waste warm water from industrial processes. The latter prefer black elvers which accept food more readily. Annual catches vary but the range is 25–60t for the

Severn. Other elver fisheries (rivers Bann, Wye, Usk, Parratt) together account for another 5–6t per annum.

Eels   The adult eel lives in a wide range of habitats throughout the British Isles, from upland trout rivers to estuaries and from drainage ditches to large eutrophic lakes. Most seaward-migrating eels (silver eels) are 9–12 years of age, having spent 3 years migrating as leptocephali and 7–10 years residing in fresh water during which time they are known as brown or yellow eels.

Before migrating, yellow eels undergo several body changes that equip them to survive in the sea. One of these involves laying down a deposit of silver pigment (guanine) below the skin surface. From August to November, silver eels descend towards the sea, and large migrations tend to occur on dark stormy nights during which time they become vulnerable to trapping. The best locations are at the

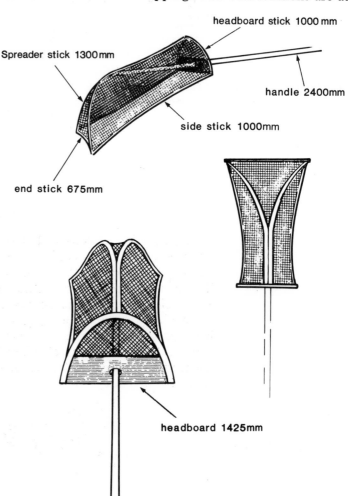

headboard stick 1000 mm

Spreader stick 1300 mm

handle 2400mm

side stick 1000mm

end stick 675mm

Fig 69 The River Severn elver net

headboard 1425mm

outlet of a lake, or at the bottom of a river system, with highest catches in tidal reaches. The fixed weir trap and wing net exploit the silver eel run, while putcheons are used to take yellow eels: fyke nets may be set to take both yellow and silver eels.

Wing nets

The wing net (*Fig 70*) has a pair of leaders to guide the eels into the net. The net itself is in the form of a long tapering sleeve with two or three inner 'non-return' valves, supported by hoops and leading to a detachable cod-end. The mouth of the net is square or circular and is kept in shape by a frame or hoop. Size varies considerably from locality to locality, but in the main River Severn fishery the nets are extremely large. They are used in the area around Gloucester where the river is about 80m wide and are set from bank to bank in order to fish the main channel. Two men and a boat are required to operate them.

Fig 70 Wing nets set in a river

Dutch fyke nets

Fyke nets (*Fig 71a*) consist of two parts, the net proper and the wing or leader. The net is conical, the opening (circular or D-shaped) varying in size from 0·25 to 1·2m in diameter and up to 4m in length. The smaller sizes are more commonly used in stillwaters for yellow eels while the larger ones are used in tidal waters for silvers. Inside the conical net are funnel traps leading to the cod-end, each trap being progressively more constrictive in aperture. The wing or leader consists of a rectangular wall of netting of about 12mm knot to knot, fastened to a head and foot rope. Wings, leaders and cod-end are staked.

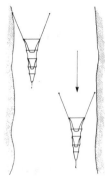

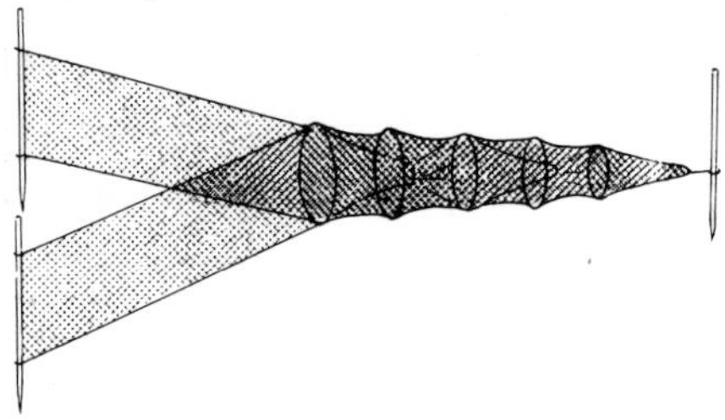

Fig 71a Fyke net

Fyke nets are commonly set in gangs (*Fig 71b*) with a pattern of leaders set out to intercept eels moving both upstream and downstream and, in the case of a lake, along the margins. Net openings may be set facing upstream, downstream or at right angles to the shoreline. In tidal waters, nets are set so as to be exposed at low tide. In non-tidal waters, cod-ends have to be lifted in order to remove the catch.

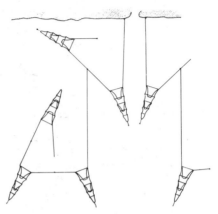

Fig 71b Fyke nets set in gangs

Putcheons

Baited eel traps, or 'putcheons' (*Fig 72*) are constructed either of withy (*Salix* spp) or, more commonly, of wire and are fairly extensively used to catch yellow and some silver eels between June and September. High river flows are preferred, and the traps may be set for about 90% of the four month period, being lifted every two to five days. Inside each trap are fitted two constricted throats through which the eel must pass to reach the bait chamber. In non-tidal reaches the putcheons are usually laid with the trap mouth upstream to catch silver eels, but in tidal reaches they can be laid facing either direction to catch eels moving up and down with the tide. Baits used are commonly animal offal, such as rabbit, or fish such as gudgeon and lamprey.

Weir traps

Many traps are now located in disused mill races rather than in weirs constructed primarily to take eels. The essential feature of all these automatic weir traps is that descending silver eels are intercepted by some form of grating and are deflected into an adjacent holding facility for collection (*see Fig 73*). Three basic types are used.

Type A: The most common trap used in abandoned mills, where it is fixed in place of the mill wheel or turbine. A sluice gate controls the level of water in the trap channel so that the upstream edge of an inclined grating is just awash. Any eels moving downstream cannot pass through the grid, but are

120

Fig 72 Baited eels traps or
'putcheons'

forced to wriggle over the top and into a trough which
eventually leads to a holding chamber. It is important that
the spacing of the grid bars should not exceed 14mm.

Type B: Although the principle and design of these traps is only a
little different from the previous type, they are much more
prone to blocking with debris. They are constructed in
ranks, with dividing walls between each.

Type C: This type is more commonly used at lake outlets, although
it could equally well be used in a disused mill. The inlet
pipe feeds directly into a holding chamber or wire basket,
preferably through a grid system to prevent clogging with
debris. The outlet pipe controls the water level in the
holding chamber.

Other traditional methods

Several other eel catching methods have been used in the past, and
some are still used today. These include 'patting' or 'bobbing' – using

121

TYPE A

THE MORE MODERN TYPE OF EEL TRAP WHICH SUPERCEDED THE OLD
TYPE OF GRID SYSTEM. THIS TYPE OF TRAP IS USUALLY INSTALLED
WHEN MILLS CEASE TO FUNCTION AS MILLS, AND THE TURBINES OR
WHEELS ARE REMOVED. THE TRAPS ARE EASY TO INSTALL AND MAINTAIN

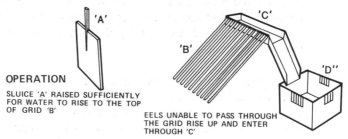

OPERATION

SLUICE 'A' RAISED SUFFICIENTLY
FOR WATER TO RISE TO THE TOP
OF GRID 'B'

EELS UNABLE TO PASS THROUGH
THE GRID RISE UP AND ENTER
THROUGH 'C'

EELS PASS ALONG THROUGH 'C'
ENTERING THE HOLDING CHAMBER 'D'

TYPE B

RIVER TEME - WORCESTERSHIRE

ALTHOUGH THE DESIGN OF THE TRAPS ON THE RIVER TEME DIFFER SLIGHTLY
TO THOSE OF THE RIVER AVON, THEY WERE EQUALLY EFFECTIVE, THEY DID
HOWEVER, REQUIRE MORE ATTENTION WHEN 'FISHING' BEING USUALLY SMALLER AND,
SUSCEPTIBLE TO BLOCKING BY DEBRIS DURING SPATE AS NO HOLDING FACILITIES
WERE INCORPORATED, SEPARATE CAGES WOULD HAVE BEEN NECESSARY.

Fig 73 This diagram shows
the three main types of
automatic eel traps

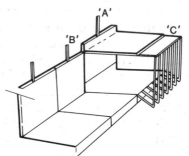

OPERATION

1. SLUICE 'A' OPENED TO ALLOW
    WATER INTO TRAP

2. EELS UNABLE TO PASS THROUGH
    GRID, REMAIN WITHIN TRAP

3. SLUICE 'B' OPENED, 'A' IS CLOSED

4. CATCH REMOVED BY MAN,
    AT APERTURE 'C'

TYPE C

VARIATIONS OF TRAPPING AND HOLDING CHAMBERS,
COMMONLY USED ON BOTH RIVER AND LAKE TRAPS

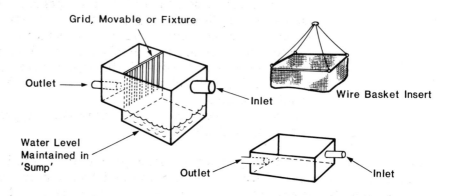

Grid, Movable or Fixture

Outlet

Inlet

Wire Basket Insert

Water Level
Maintained in
'Sump'

Outlet

Inlet

122

worms threaded onto worsted twine; 'sniggling' – using the principle of the gorge bait; baited night-lines which are legal in the tidal Severn; the putt – a large basketwork salmon trap or fixed engine (*see Fig 78*) operated in the lower Severn estuary which can be modified to take eels, flounder, mullet and shrimp; and the 'tump-net' which is a small-mesh hand net used for scooping eels from beneath overhanging banks.

Eel fishing yields and marketing

The occurrence of differing eel densities under natural conditions is primarily a function of the immigration of young fish. Superimposed on this are such factors as food availability, predation, space and cover, which govern mortality rates and ultimately production in terms of kilogrammes per hectare of marketable fish. The following statistics for yields (or total catch) are available (*Table 6*).

Table 6 EEL YIELDS FROM LAKES AND RIVERS

	Lakes (kg/ha)	Rivers (kg/ha)
High yields	10–40	20–50
Average yields	3–10	5–20
Low yields	3	5

In those lakes or rivers where eels are either absent or present in very low numbers, stocking of young 'boot lace' eels (20–50g) or elvers will lead to the development of an eel fishery. Stocking must be on an annual basis and for a minimum of ten years in order to achieve eels of a marketable size. Stocking rates of 1kg/ha of 20g eels should yield 10kg/ha; and 2kg/ha of elvers should yield 10kg/ha.

The type of eel caught is different at various times of the year. The activity of yellow eels is related closely to temperature, with peak catches occurring at the height of summer. Silver eel capture takes place in the autumn, but peak capture times vary according to distance from the sea. There is also a distinct size differentiation between males and females; the average length of males is 35–41cm and that of females is 54–61cm.

There are two distinct morphological types present in eel populations – the broad headed and narrow headed. The latter tend to have a much higher fat content and are more suited to smoking. They consequently command a premium price. Head morphology is thought to be related to diet, the broad-headed eels' food consisting mainly of fish and molluscs whereas the narrow-headed eels feed mainly on insect larvae.

European markets have definite size and quality preferences. Most eels in excess of 120g are saleable.

3.4 Commercial exploitation of salmonids

The main species of salmonid present in the British Isles – Atlantic salmon, sea trout, brown trout, rainbow trout and American brook trout – are all usually taken for food on recreational fisheries. There

123

are, however, well-established commercial fisheries for Atlantic salmon and sea trout which use different catching methods. Some of these methods are unique to specific areas of the country; others are similar to those described elsewhere in this book (Section 1.6).

This chapter will briefly describe the catching methods used by commercial salmon fisheries found near to or within the home river system of the British Isles.

The fishing instruments used can be divided into fixed and mobile types.

Fixed engines

Bag net

The bag net (*Fig 74*) may be defined as a net extending seawards from the shore, suspended from floats and anchored in a fixed position. It consists of a trap made of netting into which fish are directed by a leader, also of netting. The leader does not usually exceed 120m in length. One end of it is attached to the trap and the other securely fixed either to the shore or to a stake in the seabed. The material from which the leader is made is of sufficient thickness to be visible to the fish, and assists in directing them. No part of the trap netting should be of thinner material than the leader. Bag nets are often shot in a line extending seawards from the end of a shore-attached bag net or stake net.

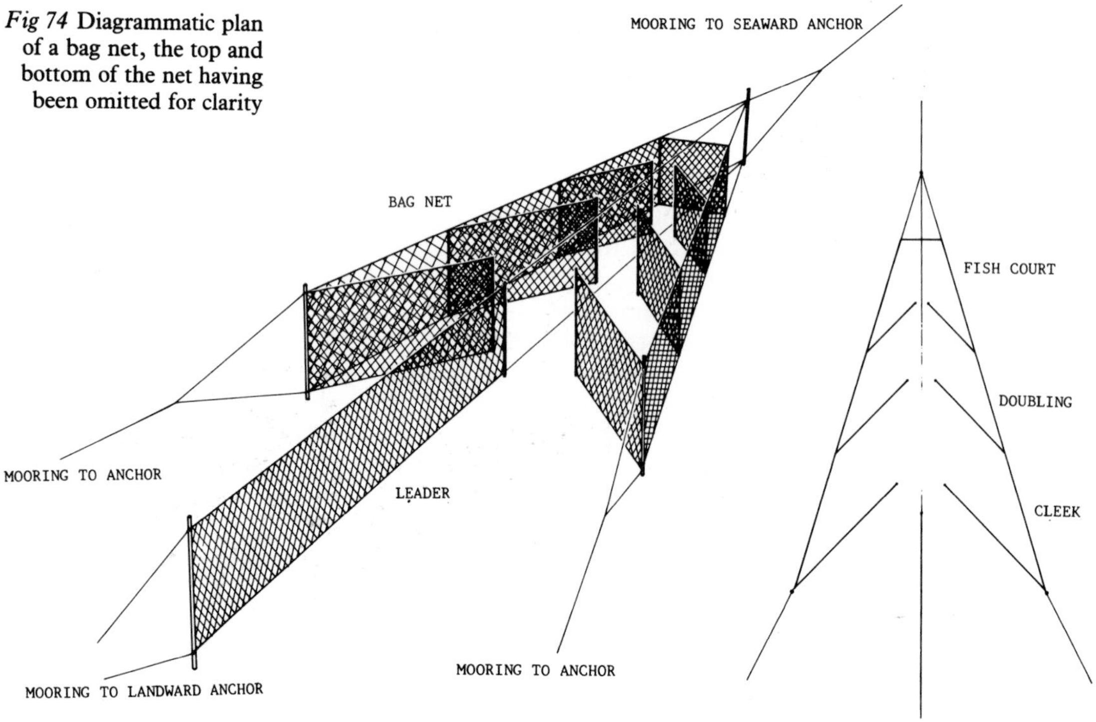

Fig 74 Diagrammatic plan of a bag net, the top and bottom of the net having been omitted for clarity

MOORING TO SEAWARD ANCHOR

BAG NET

FISH COURT

DOUBLING

MOORING TO ANCHOR

LEADER

CLEEK

MOORING TO LANDWARD ANCHOR

MOORING TO ANCHOR

124

Stake net or fly net

The stake net or fly net (*Fig 75*) is a net fixed to the foreshore by stakes. It may be defined as a curtain of netting erected on stakes and set vertically in the foreshore. It acts as a leader to approaching salmon, with a pocket or trap inserted at intervals to take fish which are directed along the leader. It is fixed to the foreshore throughout its length.

Jumper net

The jumper net is a type of fly net in which the stakes and netting of the leader are replaced by a floating curtain of netting which is fixed at both ends and which rises and falls with the tide.

Poke nets

Poke nets (*Fig 76*) are used exclusively on the Scottish side of the Solway Firth. They are mounted in lines on rows of poles and consist of a series of pockets of net in which fish are trapped and enmeshed.

'T' nets

Fig 75 The stake net, or fly net

These nets (*Fig 77*) are a development of bag nets and operate on the same principle.

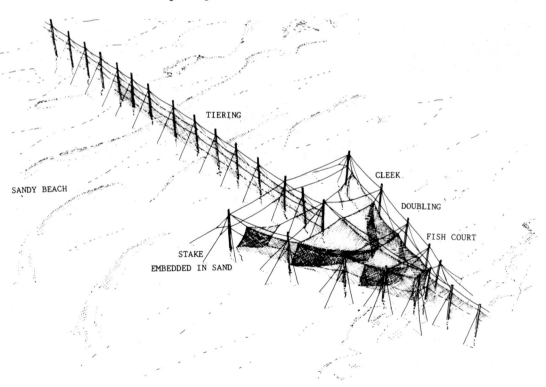

125

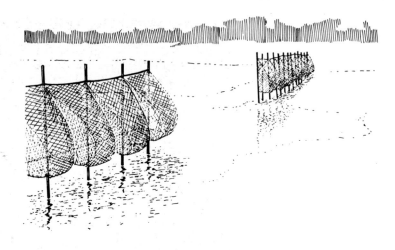

Fig 76 Poke nets

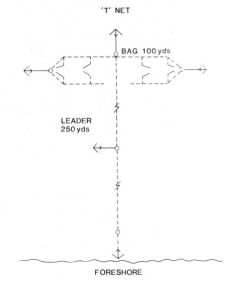

'T' NET

BAG 100 yds

LEADER
250 yds

FORESHORE

Fig 77 The 'T' net – a
development of the bag net
– in plan form

Putchers and putts

The majority of salmon caught in the Severn estuary are taken by
fixed engines, the most common of which are putchers. (*Fig 78a*).
These are typically long, conical basketwork traps (although nowa-
days some are constructed of plastic-covered steel) about 1·5m in
length and 0·6m in diameter at the opening. Several hundred may be
mounted on a framework of larch and elm poles to form a 'rank' or
fishing weir. Specific sites only can be used now for putchers,
principally those certified in pursuance of the 1865 Salmon Fishery
Act and known as 'privileged fixed engines', or occasionally those
which are lawful by virtue of grant, charter or immemorial usage,
providing they were also fishing in the open season of 1861.

126

Fig 78a Ranks of putts and putchers on the River Severn

Most putcher ranks fish the ebb tide and trap fish descending the river during their period of estuary residence before final upstream migration into freshwaters. Some ranks, however, do fish the flood tide. Efficiency of the fixed engine is greatly affected by tidal height and range.

A putt (*Fig 78b*) is a much larger trap than the putcher and consists of three separate sections – the kype, butt and forewheel. The kype (outer end) may measure 2m in diameter with the whole trap being about 4m long. Putt weirs are positioned with the mouth upstream to fish the ebb tide. Salmon, eels, dabs, flounders and shrimp are all caught in putts because of the close weave of the forewheel and butt (middle and end sections).

Stopping boats

Today, very few of these boats survive in active use. (In 1866 the Commissioners for English Fisheries issued Certificates of Privilege for 24 stop nets, but now only a few operate in the Severn and a few more in the Wye estuary). Stopping boats (*Fig 79*) are wide-beamed, stoutly built boats up to 7m in length, with a shallow draft. They are moored at right-angles to the tide, attached to a cable. A number of

Fig 78b A single row of putts and putchers

Fig 79 Stopping boats working the Severn estuary

boats may be attached to the cable in order to fish the channel, generally on the ebb tide, although there are also flood tide stations. Long poles are lashed in the shape of a 'V' with the apex inboard, and to this frame is attached a large bag net. The whole structure is finely counterbalanced and supported in the fishing position by a prop. A number of cords attached to the bag of the net are held taut by the fisherman so that he can feel when a fish hits the net. The prop is then knocked out, bringing the counterbalance into operation. The arms (raines) lift up, bringing the net opening above the water surface and trapping the fish. The end of the net is then pulled to the surface and the fish is removed and killed.

Mobile fishing instruments

Seine, draft, or net and coble

These synonyms are used in various parts of the British Isles to describe an encircling method of fishing with a net and boat (*Fig 80*). In Scotland, under the Salmon Fisheries (Scotland) Act 1868, the net and coble is the *only* method of netting permitted within the estuary limits. These limits, however, as shown in Schedule B of the 1868 Act, delineate only the seaward limits of the estuaries, and the inland waters so contained may include seawater lochs, rivers and freshwater lochs. Legal net and coble fishing must comply with certain rules which have been established by precedent in the Scottish courts. These decisions require that the net must not leave the hand of the fisherman and must be kept in motion relative to the water

Fig 80 The net and coble fishing method

129

while fishing. The construction of the net must also show that it is designed to encircle the fish and not merely to enmesh them.

The term draft or seine is applied to numerous similar fisheries in England and Wales. However, their numbers have declined substantially since the middle of the last century, almost entirely due to byelaw limitations. In the Severn, for example, draft netting extended almost as far as Welshpool on the upper reaches, but progressive curbs have limited their numbers to six in 1983, all located well below Gloucester in the tidal reach. High river flows or spring tidal velocities will often prevent successful netting by interfering with the set of the net.

Haaf nets

The haaf net (Fig 81) is restricted in use to the Solway Firth. The net is mounted on a wooden frame about 5m × 1·25m and the fisherman stands in the tide with the 'middle stick' over his shoulder and the net grounded in front of him. When he feels a fish strike the net, the frame is twisted, trapping the fish. Haaf netters frequently fish in groups, in line across the channel, on both flood and ebb tides.

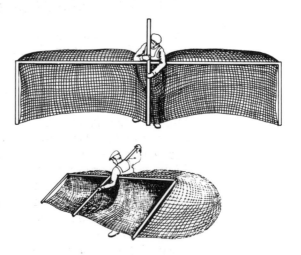

Fig 81 The haaf net, used only on the Solway Firth

Lave nets

The lave net (Fig 82) is very similar in principle to the haaf, except that the net is suspended from a collapsible Y-shaped frame about 2·5m high and with a gap of about 3m when open. Its use seems to be restricted to the Severn estuary, and there are two modes of operation. The first is similar to that employed with the haaf, but on the Severn this is known as 'lavering'; the second can only be operated under certain conditions of wind and sand configuration. It depends on the fisherman seeing the wake or 'loons' of the fish as it heads back from the receding shallow water to the low water channel. The

130

Fig 82 A lave netsman working shallow estuarine waters of the River Severn

lavenetsman then runs towards the fish, sometimes in knee deep water, and scoops it up. Fish caught in this way have been stemming the ebb or moving upstream on the ebb.

Drift nets

Drift nets consist of either a single wall or multiple walls of netting, commonly 2·5m but sometimes up to 6m deep. They are shot from a boat across the current and are allowed to drift freely. Nets are up to 370m long in most inshore and estuarine fisheries, but may be considerably longer in coastal or offshore fisheries. Single-wall nets are simple gill nets with mesh sizes ranging between 60mm knot to knot for grilse, up to 90mm knot to knot for two-, three-, or four-winter sea-fish.

Multiple-wall or trammel nets (*Fig 83*) may consist of two or three walls of netting, one of which (the lint or linnet) is made of small meshing, the other(s) (the armour) of large mesh. The principle of the trammel net is to entangle. The fish swim through the large meshes of the nearer outer wall, carrying the very loosely hung small-mesh inner netting through the larger meshes of the farther outer wall, so trapping themselves in a pocket. These nets are operable on both flood and ebb tides.

Other instruments

Several other fishing methods are used for salmon, including coracle and compass nets (Wales); stand, bow or click nets (Humber); snap,

131

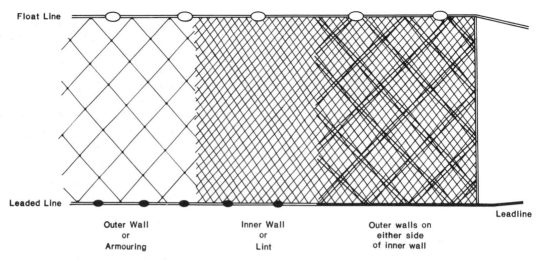

Float Line

Leaded Line

Leadline

Outer Wall
or
Armouring

Inner Wall
or
Lint

Outer walls on
either side
of inner wall

Fig 83 The trammel net, a three-walled entangling net (*From J Burgess, Trammel Netting, published by Bridport Gundry Ltd, Dorset*)

pole and hoop nets (Ireland); and channel, yair and shoulder nets (Scotland).

3.5 Aquaculture of salmonids

There are many publications for the fisheries manager to read concerning the history and development of the various aspects of aquaculture. Although it is most unlikely that any 'fish farmer' learnt from a book how to rear fish, it is hoped that the more obvious pitfalls can be avoided by the written word. This section, therefore, attempts to bring to the potential fish farmer's attention some practical advice that may make life a lot easier. It is only from practical experience on the site chosen that problems peculiar to that location will be identified.

Aquaculture in the British Isles has been, and still is, principally concerned with the rearing of salmonids. Recently, however, there has also been some development in the rearing of coarse fish such as carp and eels, and other species such as crayfish. There were approximately 500 fish farms in the British Isles in 1982. These produced about 10 000t of fish, consisting of 8 000t of rainbow trout, 1 200t of salmon, and 800t of such species as brown trout, carp, eels and flat fish. Most of these fish were for human consumption but about 10% of the rainbow trout production was for stocking recreational fisheries, as was a small additional production of brown and American brook trout.

Well-established markets exist for trout both for the table and for restocking. For the table, rainbow trout are produced in greater numbers than brown trout, and fish 20–23cm long and weighing approximately 180g, or 25–28cm long and weighing 228g, are the normal sizes sold. There is also some demand for larger fish up to 2kg. A wider size range can be sold for restocking and the higher

132

quality demanded commands a higher price. Cage-reared salmon, particularly from Scotland, are now successfully sold in the same market as commercially caught fish (*Fig 84*).

Salmonids can be reared (a) on land-based sites or (b) in floating cages. Rearing and husbandry techniques have evolved to suit the different requirements demanded in the life-cycles of rainbow trout, brown trout and salmon. *Figure 85* shows that the three species, at least in freshwater, grow at different rates. The following descriptions relate principally to the factors that should be taken into consideration when choosing a site, and also to the day-to-day routines for trout, with examples of the requirements for rearing salmon to the smolt stage where these are different.

<table>
<tr><td>

Salmonid aquaculture on
land-based sites

</td><td>

Water supply

</td></tr>
</table>

There are two main types of water supply suited to the production of trout and young salmon, namely underground or borehole water, and surface water. Borehole water generally has a temperature of 9–10°C and often contains very little dissolved oxygen. It has advantages for egg rearing in that the temperature is higher during the winter months than that normally found in rivers, thus allowing eggs

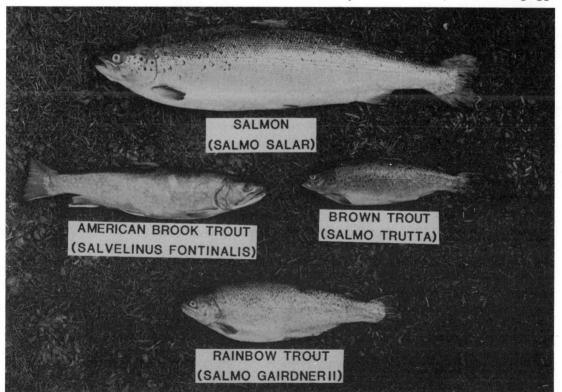

Fig 84 The four principal reared salmonids in the British Isles are the salmon, American brook trout, brown trout and rainbow trout

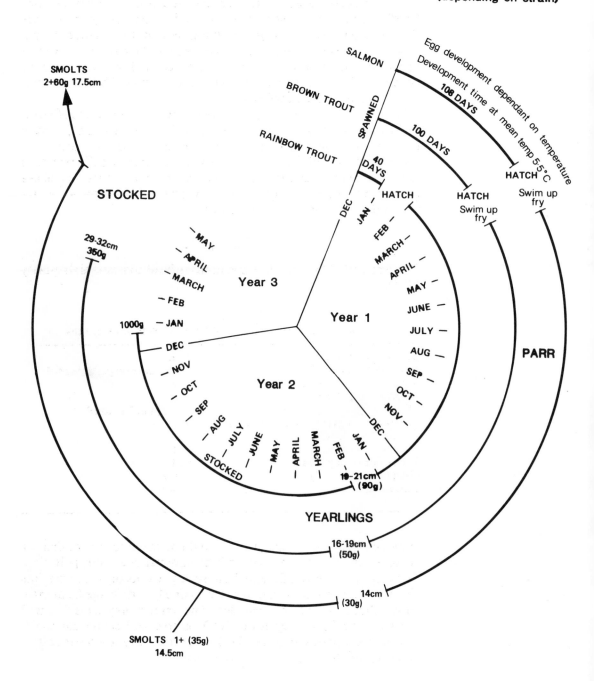

Fig 85 The rearing cycles of the principal salmonids

134

to develop more quickly. It rarely contains high levels of suspended solids, so the eggs are not smothered.

The disadvantages of boreholes are that they are costly to dig and there is no guarantee that a licence will be issued for their use. Borehole water normally needs to be pumped to the surface, and the electricity needed is expensive. The consequences of a power cut may be disastrous, and a second pump and a standby generator are therefore required as a safeguard. It is important to remember that in order to dispose of waste water, there should be a stream or water-course on, or adjacent to, the site where a fish farm is to be constructed. Spring water combines all the virtues of borehole water without some of the drawbacks.

If surface water is the main source of supply, the volume of water in the river or stream during low flows, such as prevail during a severe drought, will determine the output of fish from the farm. It is important, on a site fed by surface water, that there is sufficient drop in the level of the land to allow a gravity feed onto the site and also a gravity outfall for drainage on the downstream side. If the water has to be pumped, this can be very costly.

Water quality

The water used for trout farming needs to be of constant high quality (*Table 7*).

Table 7 WATER QUALITY REQUIREMENTS FOR TROUT FARMING

Biochemical oxygen demand	1.3
Suspended solids (mgl^{-1})	6 (increasing after rainfall)
Total oxidized nitrogen (NO_3)	2.7
Ammonia (mgl^{-1} as N)	0.1
pH	7.3 (min 7.1–max 8.3)
Electrical conductivity (micro-siemens)	432
Chloride (mgl^{-1} as Cl)	20
Alkalinity (as $CaCo_3$)	181
Total hardness (mgl^{-1} as $CaCo_3$)	224
Phosphate (mgl^{-1} as P)	0.1
Temperature °C	4–18

When choosing a site, great care should be taken to ensure that if a surface source is to be used, it is at minimal risk from pollution. Streams that receive effluents from sewage works or trade premises (including quarrying and gravel excavation), or drainage from main roads, should normally be avoided. The water supply should be well aerated, and have very little BOD or free and saline ammonia. Borehole supplies should be checked for supersaturation with nitrogen gas, which would require dispersion.

The site and locality

To accommodate the necessary ponds, access roads, accommodation and other buildings (*Fig 86*) the minimum land area required is one hectare for every ten tonnes of fish-production capacity. However, this requirement depends on the type of unit employed. The site should be free from flooding, and have an adequate fall so that all ponds can be drained individually. The security of the site against vandalism and theft is another point for consideration.

It is important to take into account the proximity of the market to potential sites, and the quality of the road system. Special equipment to transport live fish from the farm to the fisheries is essential (especially if long distances are involved) since safe transport of stock is the responsibility of the vendor. (There are, however, firms specializing in the transport of live fish).

Manpower

Fig 86 View of earth ponds at the STWA Calverton fish farm near Nottingham. Note the fixed wires to deter predatory birds

A minimum of two full-time staff is required for a 20t unit. It is very useful to have someone living on or near the fish farm to cope with emergency failures in pumps or aerators, sudden pollution, flooding, or accidental pond drainage. A person living on site also gives added security against theft or vandalism.

Some trout farmers breed from their own stock, but this is not always worthwhile for the small producer. An increasing trend is for eyed eggs (ova) or fry to be brought in from specialized suppliers.

Stripping

It is advisable to strip male and female fish under cover and in dry conditions, and this should be performed out of direct sunlight to prevent ultra-violet rays from the sun reducing egg survival rates. Some farmers strip eggs into muslin before tipping them into a dry bowl for fertilization with milt. This can prevent ovarian fluid from an overripe trout from coagulating the milt and so preventing fertilization. A 1kg trout will produce 1 500–2 000 eggs, and usually the eggs of three female trout are mixed with the milt of one male. For salmon the sex ratio may be 2:1 or 1:1, since a large female may produce many thousands of eggs and take some time to strip. Eggs and milt are then mixed with the fingers and water is added to aid fertilization. Excess milt is carefully washed away, and the fertilized eggs are left to water harden for up to one hour, after which they are counted out into trays.

From this stage onward the eggs become increasingly sensitive, and after 48 hours they should not be moved. At a temperature of 10°C, rainbow trout eggs will hatch after about 30+ days. Salmon development is slower. December eggs will not hatch until March in the south of England, and later in Scotland. Approximately halfway through their development the embryo will develop eyes, and once these are clearly visible the eggs can be handled again. At this stage the eggs are 'shocked' by shaking to sort out any unfertilized ones which become opaque and can thus be picked out. Eggs require about 20–25 litres of water per minute through each trough. Ideally it should be of good quality, free of suspended solids and with a constant temperature.

Alevins

The alevins hatch out and either drop through the egg trays or are retained, depending on the type of tray in use. There can be severe losses at this stage due to suffocation, as the alevins tend to seek cover and huddle together in corners. The baskets used for the retention of alevins are designed to provide more corners for them, thus helping to prevent suffocation.

Alevins use up their yolk sacs after a few weeks (four weeks at 10°C) and then begin rising from the bottom in search of food, hence the term 'swim up' stage. This is a very important period when they *must* be fed, and food should be offered every 20 minutes throughout the day to ensure that it is available whenever they swim up. Salmon fry begin feeding at a lower temperature than trout (about 7°C) and this can create some problems of overcrowding at indoor sites fed with borehole water and with outdoor growing-on facilities. Low outdoor temperatures may prevent an early transfer of fish from indoor tanks until later in the year. There must therefore be sufficient indoor holding capacity to cope with the fry populations until transfer to outside tanks is possible.

Fingerlings

Young fry can be grown in hatching troughs for about a further three weeks and are then usually transferred to circular or square tanks. They are stocked at high density – 20 000 fingerlings to a two-metre diameter tank with a water depth of 30cm. In the early stages this high density actually improves their feeding and growth. The water supply to the tanks should be about 120 l/min. The fingerlings are thinned out as they grow, and the water depth is increased.

Fish are stocked out from the hatchery at 12cm-plus in length. By this time, whirling disease, if present in dirt ponds, will not affect them by causing brain damage and premature death as their crania are sufficiently hard to prevent damage. Salmon parr would be 5–8cm in length by mid-summer.

Salmon

The fastest growing fish of 12·5–15·0cm will become smolts at 1+ years of age in April or May of the year following. The average weight for 1+ smolts will be approximately 35g. The smolt stage is characterized by a silvery appearance to the sides of the fish caused by the deposition of guanine on the scales. Other physiological changes occur to the fish which enable it to adapt from freshwater to seawater. Approximately 40% of salmon stock will smolt at 1+ years old. Nearly all the second-year fish should become smolts at 2+ years old. The average weight of a 2+ smolt will be 60g. Survival rate for salmon from egg to smolt is likely to be only in the order of 50–55% in ideal hatchery conditions.

Stocking densities and water supply

Ponds

Earth ponds can usually hold from 8–30 kilogrammes of trout per cubic metre, circular tanks from 30–40kg/m^3, and raceways also from 30–40 kg/m^3. The water supply has three main roles: (*i*) to supply oxygen, (*ii*) to take away waste products, and (*iii*) to support the fish. The quantity of water required per pond will vary with temperature and weight of fish present. Ten megalitres per day is the minimum amount required to produce 25t of trout in a one-pass system. Production can be increased with a two-pass system and, with full aeration, the volume of water required can be reduced by 80%. A unit producing 25 000 smolts a year will require a maximum water flow of 4·0–5·5 megalitres/day in a one-pass system.

Feeding

Trout pellets are readily available and 1·5t of food is required to produce a tonne of fish. (The actual conversion efficiency of food protein to fish protein is about 4·5 to 1, because the food has three times the concentration of protein found in fish flesh).

For rainbow trout, the average production cycle is about one year (*Fig 85*). This consists of up to two months for hatching, one month in the alevin stage, followed by nine to ten months growing to marketable size. This period may be longer in colder waters.

Grading

The individuals in a population of fish grow at vastly different rates, and grading is necessary whenever there is a marked size variation among fish grown together. Grading, however, should not be undertaken too often, since growth will be retarded and fish may be damaged. Many farmers grade only twice a year. Grading breaks up hierarchies established by dominant fish and improves feeding efficiency and growth rates because fish get the correct pellet size. Continuous market production can be achieved throughout the year because of this difference in growth rate.

Financial aspects Anyone intending to establish a new fish farm or purchase an established unit should follow the same basic financial rules for establishing any business. There are many professionals who can advise on raising the finance, and it may be worth having a consultant rather than risking financial losses.

The following observations are presented to illustrate the percentage spending on different items on a fish farm producing 25t of trout.

Typical expenditure items	*Percent*
105 000 6–8cm fish	6%
Food 37·5t	31%
Labour, one man full-time	13%
Vehicle	5%
Insurance	5%
Medication and miscellaneous	5%
Marketing, advertising *etc*	4%
Financing charges at 12% interest and repay on initial capital over 10 years	27%
Interest on working capital	4%

Income

The essence of profitable trout farming is marketing. The selling price at the farm gate or to hotels/restaurants can be 23% and 54% more than at wholesale. Selling all stock at the wrong price to the wrong market can result in a substantial loss. The time involved in the actual handling of sales must also be taken into account.

There are certain legal requirements and regulations governing the setting up of fish farms. Potential fish farmers in England and Wales need to contact their local Water Authority in relation to the following matters.

Abstraction licence

An abstraction licence is not required if the fish farm complies with all of the following conditions:

- The farm must produce fish exclusively for food.
- The water supply must be a surface (not underground) source.
- The water supply must be contiguous with the farm at the point of abstraction.

If any of these conditions do not apply, an abstraction licence is required from the Authority's Licensing Section. A new licence, or variation of an existing licence for other purposes, will require advertisement to safeguard the interests of other water users. An annual charge is payable to the Water Authority for the abstraction rights conferred by the licence. The granting of an abstraction licence does not, however, imply that the water quality is suitable for fish farming!

Impounding licence

An impounding licence must be obtained before the construction of any weir or dam takes place in a watercourse for the purpose of diverting the flow into the fish farm. The licence is required in addition to any licence for abstraction, and application is again made to the Water Authority. In certain cases where water is to be impounded, the Authority will also require a special agreement to ensure adequate protection of downstream interests. A large impoundment of more than 22·73 megalitres (5 million gallons) is subject to additional control to ensure the safety of the dam, and specialist engineering advice must be obtained from a Panel 1 Engineer appointed under the Reservoirs (Safety Provisions) Act 1930. (The implementation of the Reservoirs Act 1975 will amend the capacity of the impoundment to 25·00 megalitres).

Land drainage consents

Water Authorities have established land drainage byelaws which require consent for certain operations in or adjacent to a main river,* or any watercourse flowing directly thereto, and in the river flood plain. Such operations include erection of fences, tree planting,

---

* *The use of the term 'main river' in this context relates to the provisions of the Land Drainage Act in which certain rivers may be designated as 'main river'. It must be emphasised that quite small rivers are sometimes 'mained', and the advice of the Water Authority Land Drainage (Rivers) departments should be sought.*

disposal of rubbish, excavation affecting the bed or banks of rivers, erection of jetties and walls, *etc*. The Authority's consent is also required for the erection or alteration of any structure in, over or under a main river* which might be likely to affect the flow or impede land drainage works.

In the case of 'non-main river' watercourses, consent is required for the erection or alteration of any mill dam, weir, culvert or other obstruction to flow.

In addition to land drainage consent, consent may also be required for certain operations by Internal Drainage Boards and Local Authorities.

Consent to discharge effluent

The effluent from a fish farm falls within the definition of trade effluent for the purposes of the Rivers (Prevention and Pollution) Acts 1951–1961. (These Acts will be replaced by the Control of Pollution Act 1974 when Part II is fully implemented.) Discharge of effluent to a watercourse therefore requires the consent of the Water Authority. The quality conditions imposed on each individual discharge will be determined by the particular requirements of the receiving stream, but the following guidelines should be used:

- If possible, there should be a single outlet for the discharge, and facilities must always be provided to enable samples of the effluent to be obtained.
- Provisions may be required for measurement of the volume of water abstracted and discharged.
- The quality of the effluent discharged will be required to be substantially of the same quality as the abstracted water. The Authority's Pollution Section should be consulted for further information.
- Nothing should be added during the fish farming activities to cause the discharged effluent to be toxic to fish, fish spawn, the food of fish, or to any other river life.
- Prior to ponds being emptied or sterilized, the Water Authority should be informed in order that an officer may be present if this is considered necessary.

Under normal circumstances, all these requirements can be met by good husbandry. It should be pointed out, however, that drainage from ponds which have been in use may require settlement to reduce the suspended solids before being discharged to a stream.

Consent to introduce fish

The Salmon and Freshwater Fisheries Act 1975 forbids the transfer of any fish or fish eggs from one water to another within a Water Authority's area, or from outside the area, without written consent.

Most Authorities regard a fish farm as 'one water', but transfers between fish farms on separate sites require consent. If fish are imported from an Infected Area, as designated under the Diseases of Fish Acts 1937 and 1983, the prior consent of MAFF is required. Live salmonids may not be imported from outside Great Britain, while salmonid eggs or coarse fish imports require a health certificate and a licence from MAFF.

Planning consents

Prospective fish farmers must obtain permission from the local Planning Authority before carrying out any constructional work. Enquiries should be made from the local valuation officer on the liability to pay rates on the buildings and other works. Guidance on these matters can again be obtained from MAFF. Generally, fish farms producing for food are classed as 'agriculture', whereas those producing solely for restocking fishing waters are not.

Salmonid aquaculture in floating cages

Rearing fish in cages is a well known method in some parts of the world, particularly the Far East, but only in recent years has the practice developed in Europe, and it began mainly with the culture of salmon in the sea in Norway and Scotland. Now, most Water Authorites in England and Wales, and some commercial fish farmers, operate cage rearing units in inland and coastal waters, rearing trout for restocking and trout and salmon for the food market. Although basic husbandry techniques are the same, the method is usually cheaper than at land-based sites because the capital costs are low and no land purchase is involved. Running costs are relieved of the burden of screen cleaning, but feeding may take much longer and grading, cleaning and mending the nets are also time-consuming.

Rainbow trout are ideal fish for this type of culture and can be held at densities of up to $10kg/m^3$ in freshwater to produce acceptable fish for the restocking market. In saltwater or when rearing fish for food, as much as double this density is possible. Brown trout can also be reared, but should be stocked at no more than $6kg/m^3$.

Cage types and construction

The basic principle of a fish cage is that a floating bag net is supported at the surface by some form of flotation system and has a framework to keep it in the open position (*Fig 87*). Types vary from a simple home-made construction of polyvinyl (PVC) piping formed into a watertight square which supports the net (*Fig 88*), to a ready-made timber or metal assembly with built-in polystyrene float chambers and a walkway/working platform around the perimeter (*Fig 89*). Flotation can be achieved by using anything from polystyrene foam blocks or buoys, to oil drums or plastic containers. Different sized mesh nets are required for small fry or large fish depending on rearing requirements. The largest mesh possible should be used as this allows maximum passage of water, and the nets are also much lighter

142

Fig 87 View of a cage rearing unit at Ladybower Reservoir near Sheffield. Note the service boat, automatic feeders and storage shed

Fig 88 Simple floating cage frame constructed of polyvinyl piping

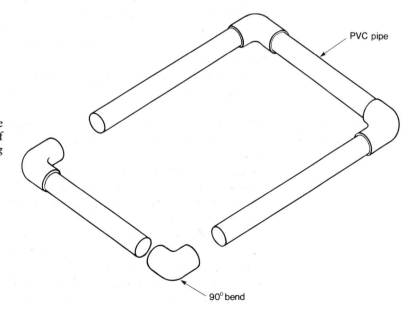

PVC pipe

90° bend

143

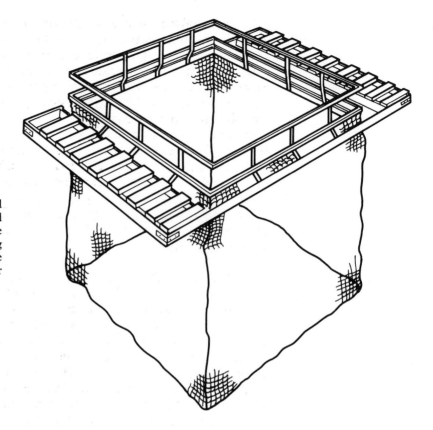

Fig 89 A typical preconstructed timber and metal frame floating cage unit, with walkway/working platform around the perimeter

OVERALL DIMENSIONS 6.1m BY 6.1m BY 4.6m DEEP
SIZE OF NET: 5.8m BY 4.6m BY 4.6m DEEP
VOLUME OF WATER ENCLOSED BY NET: 107m^3

to handle. The net needs to be weighted at the corners to keep it squarely open and to prevent it from 'riding up' in storms or strong currents.

Siting and mooring Sea cage rearing in Norway and Scotland, and more recently in Ireland, has developed successfully because of the ideal conditions in the sheltered lochs and fjords that are used as sites for cage units. Damage from storms is less likely in freshwater but as sheltered a site as possible should be chosen, particularly in larger bodies of water such as reservoirs.

If the cage is to have a rigid anchorage from two or more fixed points, then as a general guide the depth of water needs to be at least twice the depth of the cage net – that is, 6m of water would be required for a net 3m deep. Otherwise, problems will occur with a build-up of waste products on the bottom causing low dissolved oxygen levels in summer, and conditions will then be favourable for parasites and diseases.

144

In larger stillwater bodies where there are perceptible currents, the depth is not so important if the Scottish marine type of anchorage system is used: the whole unit is allowed to swing around one anchor with wind or tide. In this case it is only necessary to ensure that the water is at all times deep enough to prevent the cage snagging the bottom. Anchors can be made of concrete blocks, but such weights tend to drag under extreme strain. A better method is to use a large boat anchor or construct one with flukes that will dig into the bottom. Mooring lines should be of adequate strength, and a length of chain at the anchor end will prevent drag in much the same way as the anchor cable, rather than the anchor itself, holds a ship on station.

At smaller sites it may be easier to moor the cages directly to the shore or to build a service jetty. Specialized fish-carrying boats have also been developed to carry fish from the rearing areas to restocking or collection points.

Water quality and diseases It has been found that the more oligotrophic waters are best suited to cage rearing. Trout held in cages in lowland reservoirs or lakes with established coarse fish populations tend to become infected with parasites (particularly tape worms and eye flukes) which originate from coarse fish and reach the trout via intermediate hosts.

The water should not be subject to excessively high summer temperatures (20°C or more) for any length of time, and waters with algal blooms should be avoided. In richer, more eutrophic waters, the fouling of the nets by algae can cause problems, and may become so serious that there is no exchange of water through the cage net. This can result in fish deaths from lack of dissolved oxygen.

Routine operations With experience it will become apparent that certain routine operations are necessary for the successful operation of a cage rearing site. These will depend to a large extent on the size of the unit and where and how it is moored, but will include:

- At least one visit per day when weather conditions allow.
- The feeding of fish twice a day if possible; once in the morning and once in the afternoon, unless automatic feeders are employed.
- Correct feeding schedules. Both underfeeding and overfeeding can cause stress and affect the food conversion (2:1 is normal for cage rearing). The latter also affects the economics of the operation.
- An inspection of the mooring connections, brackets, thimbles and shackles for damage or wear at frequent intervals, particularly after heavy weather.
- The removal of any dead or dying fish for burial or incineration ashore.
- Routine hatchery or fish farm operations such as measuring and weighing samples, grading *etc* – carried out in a similar fashion as for a land-based farm.

145

- The use of divers for periodic underwater inspections of the unit.

Safety Working on a floating structure is obviously more hazardous than working on dry land, and personnel should be particularly safety-conscious. Measures to be taken to ensure safe working conditions include:

- Provision of lifebuoys for immediate use.
- The rule that lifejackets should always be worn when afloat.
- Flares or smoke signals, which should be placed on the cages so that if any person becomes marooned, he can signal for assistance.
- Informing a responsible person onshore of each visit (this is particularly important if the cages are in a secluded offshore position).
- The provision of oars on board small powered vessels in case of an engine breakdown.

3.6 Aquaculture of coarse fish

The fisheries manager could have a site and facilities that are more suited to the rearing of carp and other species of coarse fish than for trout, and the techniques for doing this are now well established.

Coarse fish farming as it is now known started with the farming of carp for food in eastern Europe and Asia. The common carp originated in the wild from the basin of the Black Sea, the Aral Sea and the Caspian, and was present in the Danube system from very early times. The construction of fish ponds in Czechoslovakia dates back to the eleventh century. This idea originated from the systematic draining and controlling of marsh areas using simple dams which created ponds suited to fish production. By the fourteenth century fish ponds were major items in the economy and were encouraged and regulated by the crown.

The breeding of the fish at this time was left to nature, but a controlled system of encouraging small numbers or even pairs of fish to spawn in small ponds was gradually evolved. This controlled breeding was a major advance as it enabled control of fry numbers and, most importantly, allowed selection of the traits required for a farmed fish. Recently, the introduction of hormone-induced spawning has allowed much finer control over brood fish and egg production. The development of artificial food for fish larvae has accelerated this control. Technically, all species of coarse fish can be farmed and the choice is governed by the market for either food or restocking.

This section presents some of the practical problems likely to be encountered, principally in carp and eel culture. A whole spectrum of methods is available for coarse fish farming, from netting a pond every two years and cropping what has grown naturally, to induced spawning and rearing on in tanks.

The rearing cycle, using carp as an example The earliest and thus most popular fish grown in Britain is the mirror carp. This is a warm-water species growing best at 28°C; it is resistant

146

to low dissolved oxygen levels, and can withstand a high level of crowding.

Pond sterilization

Ponds can be any size from 100m² for a spawning pond, to over 10ha for growing-on ponds. Typical ponds are either dug in the ground or constructed behind earth embankments. They should all be drainable and this is usually carried out by a monk system (*see Section 2.3*). The best and cheapest method of sterilizing ponds is to leave them dry and fallow over winter.

Spawning

Carp spawn at around 22°C, and the spawning ponds are prepared at the beginning of May when the water temperature is increasing rapidly. The pond is sown with grass, or other vegetation is allowed to grow, so that there is ample vegetation for the fish eggs to stick to. The ponds are empty for most of the year, but just before spawning time they are filled with water, which is allowed to warm. (These spawning ponds were originally designed by a Silesian fish farmer, Dubisch, and are normally about 10m × 10m). They are used only when the temperature of the water in them will remain above 18°C: although mature carp can withstand freezing temperatures, carp fry may die at less than 14°C. Brood fish are selected in sets consisting of two males and one female. The males are easy to recognize because milt passes from the vent when the abdomen is gently pressed; the females are identifiable at this time by their swollen abdomens and prominent vents (*Fig 90*). Carp are usually mature at four years, although males can mature earlier. The sets of fish are introduced immediately after the water has been added, and spawning takes place after about 36 hours. The females spawn on the vegetation in the centre, each fish producing around 100 000 eggs per kilogramme of body weight. The brood fish are removed immediately after spawning to prevent them from eating the eggs.

Larval stages

The carp eggs take around 100 'degree days' to hatch (thus, four days at 25°C), and the larvae measure 5mm on hatching and carry only a very small yolk sack. At or around the time of preparing the spawning pond, the nursery ponds should be made ready to receive the newly hatched larvae. Nursery ponds are bigger than spawning ponds and should be about 1·2m deep. These are used specifically for fry production and should only contain food that is of a size and quantity that can be eaten by fry. To encourage this small zoo-plankton food, the ponds are manured or fertilized. The choice lies between organic and inorganic fertilizers, and the normal organic fertilizers used are animal manure such as cow or horse manure. These can be applied at the rate of 1kg/m² in solid or liquid form, preferably at a reasonably advanced state of decay so that the ammonia level is kept to a minimum. (The level is quite variable depending on the nature of the pond soil and the existing level of nutrients in the water.) Great care must be exercised as deoxygenation can occur if too much manure is added. Rather than one large application of fertilizer, small applications should be made every few weeks during the summer.

Inorganic fertilizers can be used in place of manure, and these can create a more predictable level of algal nutrients. In normal ponds with a reasonable build-up of pond soil, it is likely that phosphorus will be the limiting nutrient so applications of superphosphate are used. A more common form of fertilizer is a 10:10:10 mixture of nitrogen, phosphorus and potassium applied at the rate of 100kg/ha with subsequent applications later in the year.

After the manure or fertilizer is added and the pond holds sufficient plankton, the newly-hatched fry are introduced. Growth is rapid at this time, and the fry must be thinned out to prevent the decreased growth rates caused by overcrowding. The fry are normally left in this pond for the rest of the season. There may also be a need for supplementary feeding if growth (checked by dip net samples) is slow. It is possible, provided the temperature is suitable, that the fish

Fig 90 View of female and male carp to show characteristic features

FEMALE

MALE

148

may 'eat out' all the naturally produced food. Pelleted food made by commercial manufacturers is the most commonly used carp food. It is nutritionally balanced for the needs of carp and can be fed to them by hand or dispensed by an automatic or demand feeder. A target weight of between 50 and 100 grammes by the end of summer is realistic if the temperature is sufficiently warm. The importance of a high temperature must be emphasized as low temperatures will result in very slow or non-existent growth. A minimum temperature for reasonable growth is 18°C, with a temperature of 23–25°C being around the optimum for food conversion and growth. The importance of temperature is such that it is economic to use solar panels, horticultural polythene tunnels, or swimming pool covers to raise the temperature of small ponds in order to promote growth.

Growing on

The cropping of ponds takes place in the autumn when growth has ceased. The fish can then be counted and graded. Some will be sold or otherwise disposed of, whilst the remainder are selected for further growth. The second and third year's growth takes place in larger ponds, up to 2ha in some cases. Stocking rates are shown in *Table 8*. The survival of the larvae to fry stage should be around 50–60% if stocking is performed carefully, adequate food is available, the temperature is reasonably high, and there are no predators. The 100g fish should, if fed, reach 600g at the end of their second year, or around 300g if there is no supplementary feeding and manuring alone is practised. The survival at this stage can be nearly 100% if care is taken as carp are remarkably robust at this size. The major problems during all of these growth phases are disease, predation and deoxygenation or pollution of the pond by the fishes own excreta.

Table 8 STOCKING RATES AND PRODUCTION FIGURES FOR CARP IN POND (*After Huismann*)

	Stocking rate fish/ha	Production target/unfed kg/ha	Production target/fed	Survival
Fry	5 000	N/A	N/A	N/A
First year	600	250	1 250	80%
Second year	200	250	1 250	90%

General husbandry

The control of disease is very largely a matter of pond hygiene. Ponds should be left dry over winter whenever possible and given a treatment of quicklime, formalin or caustic soda. Brood fish should always be kept separate from the fry and larger growing fish. Fish should be checked for parasites or other signs of disease fairly often in the growing season, preferably at least once every month. Treatment should be quick and efficacious if disease is spotted. It is important that brood fish are selected with great care so as not to bring disease onto the fish farm in the first place.

The control of predators (mainly birds and aquatic insects) is effected by exclusion rather than destruction: greenhouses are virtually predator-proof. Pollution of ponds by the fish themselves is a major problem, especially late in the season as the water warms up and the standing crop of fish is high. Deoxygenation is caused by the oxygen demand placed on the water by the fish waste products as well as by the oxygen consumption of the growing fish. This problem can be avoided by aeration during the night when the oxygen level is lowest, or by constantly changing the water, although this incurs a penalty in heat loss. The major specific pollutant killing fish in ponds is ammonia from protein breakdown products, and the situation can be made worse if the protein content of the food is too high. There is no single answer to this problem other than changing the water, but aeration helps. Keeping the pH close to neutral (7) is also effective because ammonia is ten times more toxic to fish with each single point increase on the pH scale.

This typical year of either a one, two, or three year cycle is concluded in October with pond draining and fish collection or delivery as required.

Other techniques, including induced spawning

There are a number of alternative techniques whereby various parts of the rearing cycle can be manipulated. The technique with the greatest impact has been the development of induced spawning for carp and other cyprinids. The principle of this method is to give the fish a hormone injection that mimics the hormones normally present at spawning. These hormones are obtained from dried carp pituitary glands and are injected into the fish when they are almost ready to spawn. About 18 hours after injection, the eggs can be squeezed from the female in a manner similar to that used for trout. The fish eggs are fertilized by mixing with milt, and the eggs are made non-sticky by treating them with a mixture of tannin and urea. They are then hatched out in glass vessels and the larvae introduced to tanks.

The problem at this stage becomes one of feeding the larvae, as rearing ponds are not normally available in this type of system. To overcome this, the fish are fed newly-hatched brine shrimp larvae. The brine shrimp has an encysted egg which survives desiccation and hatches in 36 hours in warm salt water. The resulting tiny brine shrimps are fed to the fish as live food for about ten days, by which time the fry can be weaned onto very small, particle-sized dry food. They can then be gradually fed larger sized food as they become bigger.

Recirculating systems

There have been many detailed investigations into the best type of

150

tank system to use in order to carry on growing the fish. The most common type is a recirculation system where the water is kept warm with artificial heat. The fish are grown in long or circular tanks and the solids in the effluent are settled in a settling tank. From the settling tank the water passes through a biological filter to oxidize the ammonia and convert it into nitrate which is non-toxic to fish. From here, the water is oxygenated and returned to the growing tank. Management of recirculating systems at high load levels is very complex, and a good understanding of water chemistry is necessary. The growth of carp in these systems can be very fast – with fish capable of reaching 1kg in less than six months.

Species other than carp All of the above techniques can, with modification and care, be used to spawn and rear fish other than carp. Recent research has shown that roach (*Fig 91* and *Table 9*) can be spawned and reared in this way. Tench, bream and rudd have also been successfully spawned, and research is continuing into these aspects of aquaculture. Grass

Fig 91 Yearling roach raised by aquaculture methods

151

carp, although not native to Britain, can be spawned and grown in the same way. In this case the adult diet can be largely vegetable matter, although pelleted food can also be used.

Table 9 STOCKING AND MORTALITY RATES FOR ROACH IN PONDS (Easton; unpublished)

	Stocking rate fish/m²	Production target kg/ha	Survival
Fry	400	N/A	80%
First year	15–20	400–500	70%
Second year	10	400–500	80–90%

Eel culture The raising of eels under controlled conditions was carried on in Japan before the beginning of this century, and later also in Europe. The best temperature for eel culture is 23–25°C, and feeding ceases altogether at temperatures below 12°C. For commercial success, eels must reach a size of 150–200g in two years. At present all the large British eel projects utilize industrial waste heat in the form of warm water. Alternative methods of heating water use solar energy by way of solar panels or greenhouses. Water supply should be of good quality and not acid. It may be clear or turbid but must not be liable to pollution. Wild eels living in the water supply are a good guide to its suitability.

It is not possible to breed eels, so farming starts with the purchase of elvers, which are obtainable from many sources in Britain, the River Severn estuary being the best known.

Elvers

Elvers are usually reared indoors in small fibre-glass or concrete tanks. Tanks similar to those used for the early stages of trout rearing are suitable.

There are appoximately 3500 elvers/kg. They should be disinfected before introducing them to rearing ponds. These are sited under cover and during the early stages the elvers are crowded, being stocked at 400g/m². As they grow they are thinned and graded, and when they reach 12g in weight they are transferred to larger outdoor rearing ponds. During the first month of elver rearing, a 20–50% mortality is common.

Later, the fingerlings are caught and transferred to adult rearing ponds. At this stage, when the eels are 20–30cm in length, many are sold to other farmers for further growth. Most eels will reach 60g in weight by the end of the first growing season and at the end of the second season they should reach a size of 150–200g, which is acceptable for the British market. A reasonable expectation would be for 1kg of elvers to yield a harvest of 400kg of market-sized eels.

152

Eels are either grown in static ponds where water exchange is minimal at 5%/day, or in higher-density systems rather like those used for trout, where water is exchanged all the time, at a rapid rate.

Outside ponds for eels can be any size from 500 to 20 000m^2 and up to 1m deep – the trend today being toward much smaller ponds. They can be excavated from soil using the spoil to create banks, and the sides are often protected with concrete slabs. All ponds used for rearing eels below 20cm in length require a lip on the edge to prevent the eels from escaping, but above this size eels rarely try to leave. Stock densities in static water ponds can be as high as 4kg/m^2.

For running water culture, ponds are much smaller; they are made from concrete and are generally circular. Stock densities are much higher at up to 10kg/m^2.

Feeding

Dry feeds for eel farming are commercially available. Generally, the feed is minced with water and oil and made into a paste before feeding. Dry food gives a conversion of 1·4:1 compared to 7:1 for wet foods. Food is placed into baskets which are lowered into the ponds. The eels swim through the mesh or climb onto the tray to get the food. Uneaten food left in the tray can be removed and thus does not foul the pond. Eels are fed usually once a day at about 8–10am during the warmest periods of the summer. The quantity of food given is about 10% of live body weight.

3.7 Crayfish farming

The native species of crayfish in this country is *Astacus Astacus* (L), but the species most commonly reared today is the signal crayfish (*Pacifastacus lenisusculus*) which is preferred because it grows faster and reaches market size in half the time of *Astacus*. It weights 20% more than *Astacus* when mature, and is reported to be resistant to the 'crayfish plague', a fungal infection.

The signal crayfish is native to western Canada and the north-western United States. In Britain, supplies can be obtained through agents, who import from Sweden where the crayfish is bred. There is a danger of bringing disease into the country with live imports, and a licence under the WLCA 1981 is required before the crayfish can legally be released into the wild. The signal crayfish can breed with the native species but produces sterile offspring.

Crayfish require a high pH – over 6 (preferably over 7) – to grow and reproduce. The ponds into which they are introduced should have a hard bottom and many suitable shelters. Water temperatures should exceed 15°C for at least three months in a year. Crayfish juveniles are brought in at the third stage in their life-cycle (after the second moult) when they are about 10mm long and independent of their mothers. They feed on aquatic plants and algae, and scavenge carrion. Juveniles should be stocked for three successive years to establish a breeding crayfish population in a pool. This ensures that there is always a range of generations capable of replacing the adult harvest which is taken annually.

The first harvest will be three years after the first stocking. Production can be as high as $1kg/m^2/yr$. The harvesting is usually carried out using small traps.

Crayfish have many fish predators, particularly eels, and before commencing rearing these should be removed from the ponds.

3.8 Other users of the aquatic environment

Natural and artificial waters are very widely utilized for leisure activities and many fishery managers will find they have to cope with several forms of recreation in addition to fishing. A description of each will give some idea of their needs and compatibility, and how they can take place at the same time and location as fishing.

Boating

Inland pleasure cruising embraces use of the inland waterway system by a variety of craft, many of which may be provided with sleeping accommodation. A wide range of boats is used, including converted narrow boats, cabin cruisers and other craft, all of which may vary considerably in size. The boats require adequate mooring facilities and these are often provided by marinas. Bankside moorings can exclude anglers from substantial stretches of bank.

Other boating activities include the occasional use of small boats by private individuals, or those hired by commercial undertakings. Access to the water is made via private or public slipways which may also provide mooring facilities.

Rowing, in an organized form, may occur on large lakes and rivers, and continues throughout the year. Most clubs organize their own regattas and head races. Rowing clubs normally own their own boats, and build or hire boathouses and club houses on the water's edge.

Canoeing has increased tremendously since 1950 with the advent of glass-fibre construction kits, and the sport can be split into three types. Canoe touring requires unrestricted passage over long stretches of river, whereas the 'white water' canoeist needs a length of rough water, normally only to be found on fast-flowing streams and rivers or below weirs or open sluice gates. Canoe racing uses lakes or rivers for a course of 1 000m or more and is conducted rather like rowing. There are some stretches of river specifically set aside for canoeists, whereas other stretches may be used occasionally with the consent of the riparian owner.

Sailing is practised on a variety of waters, and special facilities, including club houses and slipways, are often provided on reservoirs. Sailing is normally restricted to those waters that provide sufficient space for boats to tack up-wind. On large rivers with little current, they will often be forced to approach close to the bank when sailing up-wind.

Sail-boarding is a sport that has become very popular over the last

154

few years, and is carried out on virtually any water. Because the sail-boards are usually transported to and from the water on every visit, bankside access must be good. Needs are similar to sailing.

Sub-aqua Sub-aqua diving includes the use of underwater breathing equipment, face masks and simple swimming equipment. Diving takes place in reservoirs and lakes and on some rivers, but divers normally prefer those waters of high clarity and reasonable depth. Divers are normally content with a very limited area in these conditions.

Swimming Swimming is the most popular of all water-based activities. A few rivers, gravel pits and other enclosed waters are used, but seldom provide ideal conditions. Casual swimming can take place anywhere in warm summer conditions, but it is often forbidden in navigable waters. A word of warning is appropriate in that however clean a surface water looks, there is always the possibility of infection to human beings who swim there.

Water skiing Water skiing is a recent sport which has grown to its present extent in little more than 20 years. Certain inland waters are leased specifically for this activity, but there may also be water skiing zones on large rivers. Because of the noise over and under the water, and the wash created by the powerful boats needed to tow the skier, water skiing activities may cause conflict with other water users, especially if the skiers approach closer than 30m from the bank.

Informal recreation It is the quiet attractive appeal of streams, rivers and other inland waters that make them among the most valued areas for informal recreation. The popular belief in the image of cool, shady streams flowing through flowery meadows (or its upland counterpart of bubbling water dashing over rocky waterfalls) draws millions of people each year to picnic and play near water. This activity normally requires footpaths and organized or informal picnic places, which by their very nature change the environment that people come to enjoy. At worst, inconsiderate behaviour by adults and children, and lack of control of their dogs, can disrupt other activities such as angling, which require quiet.

Nature conservation Many of the water resources suitable for recreational use also have considerable scientific, environmental or educational value because of the plant and animal life they support. Conservation bodies are therefore particularly concerned to ensure that all forms of water recreation have particular regard for the environment.

155

Appendix 1

Administration of freshwater fisheries in the British Isles

All inland waters are owned by somebody, and fishing rights may be owned together with the land on which the water is situated, or separately from the ownership of the land. However, the situation varies in different parts of the British Isles, although the individual rights of an owner will be recorded in the deeds of the property. Scottish law is based on a different system from that of England and Wales, although much of it is the same and the ultimate Court of Appeal for all is the House of Lords. Northern Ireland is subject to many of the laws of England and Wales although there are local provisions. The Republic of Ireland has its own legal system.

The administration of an individual fishery will vary depending on whether it is being used for angling or for commercial fishing. This is usually left to the needs of the owner. The management operations undertaken by the fishery owner will be influenced by the common and statute law of the country and how fisheries legislation is administered at national and/or local level.

Scotland

In Scotland the right of salmon fishing and sea trout fishing derives from the Crown. There are no public fisheries and all salmon and sea trout fishing is privately owned, both in inland rivers and the sea out to the limit of territorial waters.* Those fisheries which have been the subject of a grant to a member of the public in times past are heritable property and may be separated from the land in riparian ownership. The Secretary of State for Scotland has overall responsibility for salmon and freshwater fisheries, whilst the Fisheries Division of the Department of Agriculture and Fisheries for Scotland is the central administrative body for these fisheries.

Local administration and statutory protection of salmon fisheries is carried out by Salmon District Fishery Boards. A district nearly always comprises the individual catchment of a river system, and

---

* The limit of territorial waters in relation to seaward boundaries of Water Authorities for the purposes of Fisheries Functions is described in Schedule 2(4) of the Water Act 1973, as 'shall include those tidal waters and parts of the sea adjoining the coast of the water authority area in which Her Majesty's subjects have the exclusive right of fishing'. (*ie* 6 nautical miles from the base line).

156

extends for a certain distance along the coast on either side of the river mouth. A District Board may appoint water bailiffs to enforce the Scottish salmon laws but it has no powers in respect of brown trout or other species of freshwater fish. There is no official fisheries administration at local level for species other than salmon and sea trout.

Scottish District Boards are empowered to impose a fisheries rate on the proprietors of salmon fisheries, both in rivers and in the sea within their districts. A Board decides its own level of rating according to its means. Board members are elected solely from salmon fishery proprietors and the proprietor with the highest rateable value is automatically the Chairman of the Board.

Northern Ireland There are no bodies analogous to the English and Welsh Regional Water Authorities in Northern Ireland. The various components of the Water Industry are divided between several Government departments and statutory bodies.

The Department of Agriculture for Northern Ireland has overall responsibility for fisheries and land drainage. The Fisheries Department has two main sections: the first is responsible for administrative matters such as policy and finance; the second is responsible for professional and technical matters related to the development of public angling, sea fisheries, the Department's salmonid culture centre and a specific long-term investigation into salmon population dynamics (which incorporates a smolt rearing unit). Fish farming is regulated by the Department with a system of licences and grants and loans for their development.

Fisheries protection and law enforcement are the responsibility of two statutory bodies – the Fisheries Conservancy Board which covers the larger part of the Province, and the Foyle Fisheries Commission covering the whole catchment of the River Foyle (part of which lies in the Republic of Ireland).

Republic of Ireland The Department of Agriculture and Fisheries promote the development of all activities related to inland fisheries. It is responsible for the allocation of finance to a number of other organizations concerned with such matters and also for initiating research into various aspects of fisheries. It also manages over 100 state-owned fisheries, including a number of hatcheries.

The 1848 Fisheries Act laid the foundation for the present system of administration of inland fisheries. Today, administration is primarily in the hands of 17 Boards of Conservators who are elected by various fishery interests every four years.

The functions of the Boards of Conservators are summarized briefly as follows:

• To appoint staff for the protection, conservation and improvement of the fisheries and to implement the provisions of the Fisheries Act.

- To administer the fishery Acts in relation to pollution.
- To instigate public sworn enquiries for the passing of byelaws for the improvement or control of fisheries.

The Boards are also responsible for collecting their own revenue from fishing licences and a rate on the list of valuations for the fishery district.

The Inland Fisheries Trust is a registered company set up by the Government in 1951 for the promotion and development of trout and coarse fisheries throughout the country. Its responsibilities also extend to sea angling. Membership of the Trust is open to all anglers for a small annual membership fee. The Trust is essentially a non-profit-making organization, all of whose income is devoted to fishery development work and research.

The Salmon Research Trust of Ireland was set up in the 1960s, and its activities are directed towards the selective breeding of salmon and sea trout.

The Electricity Supply Board (ESB) owns the fishing rights on all its reservoirs, and on certain sections of the rivers (excluding R. Shannon) that have been developed for hydro-electric purposes. It operates three hatcheries and rearing stations. Fisheries research also forms an important part of the ESB work.

England and Wales An explanation of how freshwater fisheries are administered in England and Wales is contained in the Salmon and Freshwater Fisheries Act 1975. Section 28 states that it shall be the duty of every Water Authority to maintain, improve and develop the salmon fisheries, trout fisheries, freshwater fisheries and eel fisheries in the area for which they exercise fisheries functions. They must also establish advisory committees of persons who appear to them to be interested in any such fisheries in that area, and consult them as to the manner in which the Authority is to discharge its duty.

All ten Water Authorities employ fisheries staff of various types of specialization to discharge this duty. They are also responsible for issuing fishing licences (for angling or commercial purposes), the revenue from which contributes towards the costs incurred by the fisheries service. Responsibilities also extend to include most professional, technical and legislative matters related to fisheries. The fisheries function is generally managed by Water Authorities as one of the many integrated facets of the water cycle.

The Ministry of Agriculture, Fisheries and Food has a specific interest in fisheries from the food production aspect. In particular, it has specific duties in some aspects of legislation related to licensing and fishery byelaw approvals, technical matters related to fish farming, and fish disease diagnosis and research.

Appendix 2

Careers in freshwater fisheries The Institute of Fisheries Management provides detailed advice on careers in freshwater fisheries, and has described a simple generalized career structure, applicable to most of the major employers in this country (*Fig 92*).

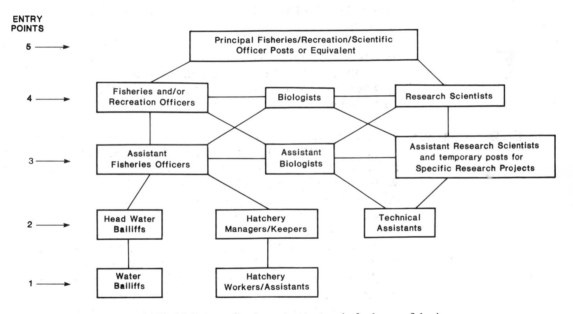

Fig 92 A generalized career structure in freshwater fisheries

Five entry points are distinguished.

Point 1: A general interest in fisheries. Previous experience of fishing methods, dealing with anglers and police work, is useful for the Water Bailiff positions. The Certificate of the Institute of Fisheries Management is an advantage.

Point 2: For the Head Bailiff and Hatchery Manager/Keeper positions, experience of working in a post at Point 1 is the major

159

requirement. For the Technical Assistant posts, relevant 'O' and 'A' Level GCE certificates (or equivalent) are normally required, and further qualifications are an advantage.

Point 3: Experience in a relevant post at Point 2 or a degree in a biological subject coupled with other relevant experience is expected. Postgraduate experience is particularly useful for the research posts. The Diploma in the Institute of Fisheries Management is an advantage.

Point 4: Experience in a relevant post at Point 3 would be expected, or a higher university degree in a biological subject coupled with a number of years of involvement in the fisheries field.

Point 5: A university degree coupled with several years of working in a relevant post at Point 4 is a minimum requirement.

Major employers include the Regional Water Authorities, MAFF, CEGB, various research organizations (such as the FBA: *See Appendix 3*), some Universities, and fish farms (although many are small).

Further training at various levels is offered by the Institute of Fisheries Management; The Hampshire College of Agriculture, Sparsholt, near Winchester; A Behrendt, Two Lakes, Romsey, Hants; Institute of Aquaculture, University of Stirling, Stirling; Department of Applied Biology, University of Wales Institute of Science and Technology (UWIST), Cardiff; School of Maritime Studies, Plymouth Polytechnic, Plymouth.

Most jobs are advertized in the national press, and the NFU maintains a register of members interested in fish farming and those seeking jobs in fish farming.

Appendix 3

The aim of this appendix is to provide an A–Z guide to the many organizations with whom a fisheries manager may come into contact, or may wish to consult.

Anglers' Co-operative Association (ACA) address: Midland Bank Chambers, Westgate, Grantham, Lincs NG21 6LE.

The Association is concerned with handling, on behalf of its members, cases of pollution resulting in fish mortality, and with obtaining an acceptable level of compensation for their members.

British Waterways Board – Recreation and Amenities (BWB) address: Willow Grange, Church Road, Watford, Herts.

The Fisheries Department of British Waterways Board is responsible for fisheries in its own canals and reservoirs. It sets the level of any rental fees, and may undertake stocking.

Central Council for Physical Recreation (CCPR) address: Francis House, Francis Street, London SW1 1DE.

This is a national body, supported by Sports Council grant, which provides a forum for the governing bodies of sport at national level. It has six specialist divisions, one of which is water recreation.

Countryside Commission address: John Dower House, Crescent Place, Cheltenham, Glos GL50 3RA.

The Commission offers expertise on all matters relating to the conservation of the landscape; provision of facilities for informal countryside recreation; the management design, and development of countryside information; and interpretation services and facilities.

The Commission was set up in 1968 under the Countryside Act. Its principal functions are aimed at the conservation and enhancement of the natural beauty of the countryside, and it encourages the provision and improvement of facilities for public enjoyment of the countryside and of open air recreation.

Country Landowners' Association (CLA) address: 16 Belgrave Square, London SW1X 8PQ.

This is the central association of country landowners, many of whom are also riparian owners of fisheries and have a keen interest in the maintenance and improvement of fisheries generally. The Association is concerned to protect lands and fisheries against harmful developments and to achieve the best deal possible for members when such projects as new trunk roads *etc* are being considered at national or local level.

Development Board for Rural Wales address: Ladywell House, Newtown, Powys.

Forestry Commission address: 21 Corstorphine Road, Edinburgh EH12 7AT.

This is the organization responsible for the promotion of forestry resources generally, including afforestation development, the establishment and maintenance of adequate reserves of growing trees, and thus the production and supply of timber.

Freshwater Biological Association (FBA) address: Ferry House, Far Sawrey, Ambleside, Cumbria.

The Association conducts research into all aspects of freshwater biology, and has performed many short and long-term studies on various species of freshwater fish and their food. The main laboratory is on Lake Windermere, with a river laboratory at East Stoke, Dorset.

Highlands and Islands Development Board address: Bridge House, Bank Street, Inverness, Scotland.

Inland Waterways Amenity Advisory Council address: 122 Cleveland Street, London W1P 5DN.

The Council is a statutory body set up in 1968. It represents the interests of all types of users on the canal and river network of the BWB.

Institute of Biology address: 20 Queensberry Place, London SW7 2DZ.

This is a professional institute for all types of biologists. It has comprehensive training courses leading up to Degree and other levels of qualification.

Institute of Fisheries Management (IFM) address: Balmaha, Coldwells Road, Holmer, Hereford.

This is the professional body of fisheries management. Its aims are to promote the profession and to improve the status and efficiency of its members. To this end it operates a training course leading to professional qualifications at intermediate and higher level. The Institute is organized into local branches which roughly correspond with Regional Water Authority areas.

Institute of Water Pollution Control (IWPC) address: Ledsun House, 53 London Road, Maidstone, Kent ME16 8JH

This is the professional body of water pollution control.

Ministry of Agriculture, Fisheries and Food (MAFF)

Various branches of the Ministry are involved in different aspects of fisheries. At Great Westminster House, Horseferry Road, London SW1, are located the sections that deal with proposals for variation of licence duties and objections thereto, and with confirmation of varied, or new fishery byelaws.

At Lookout House, The Nothe, Weymouth, Dorset, is the Ministry's fish diseases laboratory. The laboratory is equipped to identify all known types of fish disease of a transmissible nature, whether bacterial or viral, and carries out research in addition to providing a pathological examination service to Authorities. The MAFF laboratory at Lowestoft has overall responsibility for all freshwater and marine operations. The Director of fisheries research is based there.

National Anglers' Council (NAC) address: 5 Cowgate, Peterborough, Cambs PE1 1LR.

This is the national representative body for angling of all types with which Central Government consults on all matters relating to the sport and policy affecting it. The National Federation of Anglers which, prior to the establishment of the Council was regarded as the national body for freshwater angling, is represented on the Council.

National Association of Specialist Anglers (NASA) address: 5 Silvercourt, High Street, Brownhills, Walsall, West Midlands.

The Association exists to protect and promote the interests of those anglers seeking larger than average fish. Membership includes individuals, specimen groups and the 'single species' groups (*eg* Pike Anglers Club). It organizes the Annual British Angling Conference.

National Commercial Salmon Netsmen's Circle of the Fisheries Organization Society Ltd address: New Fish Quay, Brixham, Devon

This is the central association of salmon netsmen in Britain, and it is concerned with all matters which may affect the interests of netting on rivers and estuaries.

National Farmers' Union (NFU) address: Agriculture House, Knightsbridge, London SW1X 7NJ.

This Union was set up in 1908. Its basic role is described as to provide the circumstances in which British farmers and growers are able to pursue their business effectively, on fair terms, and without undue pressure or interference. It represents 85% of full-time farmers in England and Wales, and has an active fish farming section.

National Federation of Anglers (**NFA**) address: Halliday House, 2 Wilson Street, Derby DE1 1PG.

This is the governing body of coarse angling in Britain, and deals with all aspects of the sport. It also organizes the running, annually, of the National Angling Championship in the several divisions into which affiliated clubs are divided.

Natural Environment Research Council (**NERC**) address: Polaris House, North Star Avenue, Swindon, Wilts 5NZ 1EV.

NERC is responsible for encouraging, planning, funding and executing research in those physical and biological sciences that relate to the natural environment and its resources.

Nature Conservancy Council (**NCC**) address: 19/20 Belgrave Square, London SW1X 8PY.

This Council is financed through the Department of the Environment and its principal functions are the establishment and management of nature reserves in Great Britain; the provision of advice to Government ministers and others; the dissemination of information about nature conservation; and the commissioning of relevant research. It is the statutory body responsible for nature conservation in Britain.

Regional Water Authorities addresses: see below.

There are ten RWAs in England and Wales covering the areas shown in *Figure 8*. They have a clear duty to fisheries, described in Appendix 1, and have a duty to make the best use of their waters for purposes of recreation.

Anglia WA	Diploma House, Grammar School Walk, Huntingdon PE18 6NZ.
Northumbrian WA	Eldon House, Regent Street, Gosforth, Newcastle-upon-Tyne NE3 3PX.
North-West WA	Dawson House, Great Sankey, Warrington WA5 3LW.
Severn-Trent WA	Abelson House, 2297 Coventry Road, Sheldon, Birmingham B26 3PU.
Southern WA	Guildbourne House, Worthing, Sussex BN11 1LD.
South-West WA	PO Box 22, 3–5 Barnfield Road, Exeter EX11 1RE.

Thames WA	Reading Bridge House, De Bohun Road, Reading, Berks.
Welsh WA	Cambrian Way, Brecon LD3 7HP.
Wessex WA	Techno House, Redcliffe Way, Bristol BS1 6NY.
Yorkshire WA	West Riding House, 67 Albion Street, Leeds LS1 5AA.

Salmon and Trout Association (STA) address: Fishmongers' Hall, London Bridge, London EC4R 9EL.

The Association is concerned with the well-being of game fishing throughout Britain, and maintains contact with Central Government on matters affecting the sport directly or through proposed legislation.

The Sports Council address: 16 Hoburn Place, London.

This is an independent body which was established in 1972 by Royal Charter. It has wide executive powers and overall responsibility for matters concerning British sport. Besides dispensing grant aid, it has extensive promotional and advisory functions.

Weed Research Organisation (WRO) address: Begbroke Hill, Yarnton, Oxford OX5 1PF.

The Aquatic Weeds Section is concerned with research into herbicides and other methods of controlling weed growth in freshwater, both static and running. Much of the work done is of use in dealing with fishery management problems involving weeds.

Appendix 4

Fisheries grants Various organizations provide grants for fishery development operations. The following is a list of organizations which angling club secretaries might wish to approach.

Regional Water Authorities Some Authorities offer up to 50% of the total cost of any scheme that physically improves a fishery. Such improvements must generally create more fishing space for anglers, and waters improved must be available to day ticket anglers. Details can be obtained by writing to the Principal Fisheries Officer at one of the addresses in Appendix 3.

Sports Council Details of Sports Council grants can be obtained from the local divisional offices. Grants or interest-free loans may be offered towards the reasonable capital cost of providing essential facilities for those taking an active part in sport: purchase of fishing rights is one example. A grant may be given of up to 50% of the approved cost of the project as valued by the District Valuer. The maximum value of a Sports Council grant is £20 000.

Countryside Commission Details of grants for private individuals and bodies are set out in a leaflet by the Commission (CCP 79). Grants can be made in respect of any expenditure which the Commission considers conducive to the conservation and enhancement of the natural beauty of the countryside, and the provision and improvement of facilities for the enjoyment of the countryside and for open-air recreation.

Grants for fish farming Grants are available for the commercial production of freshwater fish for food under the Farm and Horticultural Development Scheme (FHDS), but only those who are already in business in farming or horticulture may apply. Further details can be obtained from the socio-economic advisers at the MAFF divisional offices.

For those ineligible for FHDS, grant aid may be available from the EEC Agricultural Fund (FEOGA). This grant is mainly for co-operative proposals between several fish farms on projects exceeding

166

£75 000 in total (1981 baseline). Applications should again be made via MAFF.

Finally, a selective assistance scheme is available from the Department of Industry only for farms in development areas ineligible for the FHDS grant.

The Development Board for Rural Wales and the Highlands and Islands Development Board also provide grants for fish farming.

Tree planting grants Whether or not grants are available depends very much on the scale of the planting scheme. Grants are not likely to be made for a handful of trees, but if the area involved is large enough, or if the planting can be incorporated into a larger scheme, then grants may well be payable. The Forestry Commission or your local County Council should be contacted for further information. Before planting trees around your pool or alongside the river, make sure that the riparian owner is agreeable and – if it is a watercourse – check that the Land Drainage Department of the Water Authority has no objection. The department may require one tree-free bank from which to carry out maintenance work, and their bye-laws commonly regulate tree planting near watercourses.

Appendix 5

Legislation for angling club administrators

It is outside the scope of this appendix to attempt to describe the role and function of the many government departments and authorities who control or operate the following Acts of Parliament. It is therefore useful to include on the Club Committee, a person or persons with some expertise in financial and legal matters. The following notes give just the briefest outline of the essential elements of some of the relevant statutes.

Salmon and Freshwater Fisheries Act 1975

This deals with the fishery functions of Water Authorities. It also consolidated into one statute the previous six Salmon and Freshwater Fisheries Acts.

The Act, in addition to those duties described in Appendix 1, also controls the methods of fishing, the close seasons during which fishing may not take place, and in certain circumstances the size of fish which may be lawfully caught. It covers the licensing of users, the administration and reinforcement of the Act, and movement and introduction of fish into inland waters. It also gives Water Authorities powers to make byelaws.

Diseases of Fish Acts 1937 and 1983

These Acts enable the Minister of Agriculture, Fisheries and Food to take measures to control the spread of disease by making certain diseases 'notifiable'. The Acts also control the importation of live fish and the eggs of fish.

Where a Water Authority suspects that any waters are infected with any disease of fish to which the Acts apply, it must report it to the Minister. In an 'infected area', the Minister may authorize the Water Authority to remove dying or dead fish from that 'infected area', but this does not apply to fish farms. The Acts do not enable the Minister to pay compensation as it would in the case of some diseases of cattle requiring animals to be slaughtered.

Theft Act 1968

Schedule 1, paragraph 2 of the Theft Act 1968, deals specifically with taking or destroying fish from private property.

(*1*) Subject to paragraph (*2*) below, a person who unlawfully takes or destroys, or attempts to take or destroy, any fish in water which is private property or in which there is any private right of fishery is liable on summary conviction to a fine not exceeding £50 or, for an offence committed after a previous conviction for an offence under this paragraph, to imprisonment for a term not exceeding three months or to a fine not exceeding £100 or to both.

(2) Paragraph (1) above does not apply to taking or destroying fish by angling in the daytime (ie in the period beginning one hour before sunrise and ending one hour after sunset), but a person who by angling in the daytime unlawfully takes or destroys, or attempts to take or destroy, any fish in water which is private property or in which there is any private right of fishery is liable on summary conviction to a fine not exceeding £20.

(3) The court by which a person is convicted of an offence under this provision may order the forfeiture of anything which, at the time of the offence, he had with him for use in taking or destroying fish.

(4) Any person may arrest without warrant anyone who is, or whom he, with reasonable cause, suspects to be, committing an offence under paragraph (1) above, and may seize from any person who is, or whom he, with reasonable cause, suspects to be, committing any offence under this provision anything which on that person's conviction of the offence would be liable to be forfeited under paragraph (3) above.

Under paragraph (2) the maximum penalty is £20.* Angling at night, and taking or attempting to take and destroy fish by any method (other than angling during the day) during the night or during the day, the maximum penalty is £50.* The power of arrest without warrant does not apply to angling during the day time. The Theft Act 1968 stopped the 'apparent right' of owners, club bailiffs and gamekeepers from confiscating fishing tackle instead of going to court.

Reservoirs (Safety Provisions) Act 1975   The Reservoirs Act 1975, with powers to make regulations and orders, will replace the 1930 Act in a series of stages. Phase 1 of the 1975 Act is scheduled to become operative in late 1984; Phase 2 is scheduled for October 1984; Phase 3 for October 1985.

A large reservoir, any part of which is above the level of the adjacent ground and which has a capacity for holding in excess of 5 million gallons (22.7 megalitres) (under the 1930 Act), will require periodic inspection by a qualified (Panel 1) civil engineer. A qualified civil engineer must also design and supervise the construction or enlargement of a reservoir, which can only then be filled in accordance with his certificate.

---

* The Criminal Law Act 1977 increased fines under many statutes (one was the Salmon and Freshwater Fisheries Act), but it does not appear to have increased the fines under Schedule 1 of the Theft Act.

National Parks and Access to the Countryside Act 1949 and Countryside Act 1968

This gives power to the local Planning Authority to enforce access to a public path and to stop notices deterring the public from using footpaths. It also gives the Authority powers of entry upon land for the purpose of surveying the land.

Section 119 of the **Highways Act 1959** refers to ploughing of footpaths or bridgeways, and gives the duty of enforcing provisions under the Act to the Highway Authority.

Rivers (Prevention of Pollution) Act 1951–1961

The control and prevention of pollution of rivers is the responsibility of the Water Authorities. Part 2 of the Control of Pollution Act 1974, which was passed on 31 July 1974, will replace and repeal the Pollution Acts of 1951–1961 on a date to be set by the Secretary of State for the Environment.

It is an offence for a person to cause or knowingly permit any poisonous, noxious or polluting matter to enter a stream.

It is an offence, except with the consent of the Water Authority, to cause a deposit accumulated from a dam, weir or sluice to be carried away in the water of a stream when cleansing the channel, or wilfully and without consent to allow a substantial amount of cut or uprooted vegetation to remain in the stream. Byelaws can be made by the Water Authority.

Protection of Birds Act 1954 and 1976 (Incorporated into Wildlife and Countryside Act 1981)

The 1954 Act sets out in four schedules; (*1*) birds which are protected at all times and during the close season; (*2*) wild birds which may be killed or taken at any time by authorized persons; (*3*) wild birds which may be killed or taken outside the close season, and (*4*) wild birds which may not be sold alive unless close-ringed and bred in captivity.

Section 8 of the 1976 Act would appear to allow a licence to kill birds to prevent serious damage to property or to fisheries.

Water Resources Act 1963

The Act is to promote measures for the conservation, redistributing, augmenting and securing the proper use of water resources or of transferring those resources to another area. A person who abstracts water from a watercourse or underground strata requires a licence to abstract. The construction or alteration of impounding works in a watercourse also requires a licence. The owner of a fishery can, under certain circumstances, apply for an existing licence to be revoked where he can prove damage or loss due to an existing abstraction. The erection of a culvert in a watercourse, or the alteration or removal of any mill dam, weir or other like obstruction requires consent of the water authority.

Health and Safety at Work Act 1974

It is the duty of every employer to ensure, so far as is reasonably practicable, the health, safety and welfare at work of all his employees. He must provide and maintain a working environment for his employees that is, so far as is reasonably practicable, safe, without risks to health, and adequate as regards facilities and arrangements for their welfare at work.

The Health and Safety Executive issue many guidance leaflets, and enquiries should be made direct to Baynards House, 1 Chepstow Place, London W2.

Sex Discrimination Act 1975 This Act is designed to promote equality of opportunity between men and women, and to render certain kinds of sex discrimination unlawful. It is largely enforceable by taking civil proceedings. The fisheries administration must be aware of the above statute prior to advertising for staff.

Drought Act 1976 Any person who takes or uses water in contravention of a prohibition or limitation order, or discharges water contrary to any condition or restriction commits an offence. An order may be made to measure the flow of water and keep records.

Land Drainage Act 1976 The purposes of land drainage can be summarized as the protection of life, land, urban areas and property from flooding; the improvement of agricultural land; and the conservation of water for riparian use. Nothing in the Land Drainage Act 1976 can affect or prejudice the provisions of the Salmon and Freshwater Fisheries Act 1975, and due regard must be taken of fishery interests. A Water Authority must exercise a general supervision over all matters relating to land drainage in its area.

Internal drainage boards were not affected by the 1976 Act. Water Authorities have powers to make byelaws for such things as planting of trees by watercourses, blocking of watercourses *etc*.

Wildlife and Countryside Act 1981 In England and Wales the release into the wild, whether deliberately or unintentionally, of any fish or shellfish not ordinarily resident in Great Britain, or which is listed in Schedule 9 to the WLCA 1981, or the eggs of such fish or shellfish, is an offence unless the release has been authorized by an individual licence issued by the MAFF or the Welsh Office Agriculture Department. An individual licence, for which a fee will be payable, will cover the release of a single consignment into one location and will be granted if, after consultation with the Nature Conservancy Council and the appropriate Water Authority, the Minister or Secretary of State for Wales is satisfied that the introduction is justified. Releases of fish into totally enclosed ornamental lakes and ponds and fish farms are outside the scope of the Act, although the permission of Water Authorities is still required.

The aim of this licensing scheme is to control the release of new or non-native species of fish (including shellfish) into the wild because of their effect on the indigenous flora and fauna. The fish that are established in the wild in some parts of the country, and listed in Schedule 9 to the Act, are large-mouthed black bass, rock bass,

171

bitterling, pumpkinseed (othertwise known as sun-fish or pond-perch), wels (otherwise known as European catfish) and zander.

Details and application forms are available from the Ministry of Agriculture, Fisheries and Food, Fisheries IA, Room 368, Great Westminster House, Horseferry Road, London SW1P 2AE, or, for the Welsh Water Authority area, the Welsh Office Agriculture Department, Cathays Park, Cardiff CF1 3NQ.

Section 14 of the Act prohibits the introduction into the wild of animals, including fish and shellfish, which are not ordinarily resident in and are not regular visitors to Great Britain, while section 16 provides an exemption to section 14 if a licence is granted by the appropriate authority.

Under the Act the appropriate authority is:

(1) in relation to fish and shellfish in England and that part of the area of the Severn-Trent Water Authority in Wales, the Minister of Agriculture, Fisheries and Food.
(2) in the case of salmon and freshwater fish in the area of the Welsh Water Authority and sea fish and shellfish off the coast of Wales, the Secretary of State for Wales.
(3) in the case of fish and shellfish in Scottish waters, the Secretary of State for Scotland.

These provisions of the Wildlife and Countryside Act 1981 do not extend to Northern Ireland.

The Judges' Rules
These describe the correct manner of collecting evidence for prosecution – in effect, the 'dos' and 'dont's'.

Occupiers Liability Act 1957
The occupier of premises owes to all visitors the duty to take such care as is necessary to see that the visitor (invitees and licensees) will be reasonably safe in using the premises for the purpose for which he is invited or permitted to be there. In some cases this may even apply to trespassers (*see below*).

The occupier has a duty to ensure that the condition of the premises is reasonably safe and a duty to ensure no dangerous activity is carried on in his premises.

Trespass
A person who enters upon another's land without his consent or acquiescence, or without lawful authority, is trespassing. Trespass to land is interference with the possession of land. Where land and water is leased to an angling organization, it is the leasing anglers that have possession, not the owner of the land. It is not necessary for the plaintiff to show actual damage in order to commence proceedings in a civil court. It is possible to obtain an injunction without proof of damage.

It is suggested that if a trespasser is found, he should first be made

172

aware of his trespass; he must then be asked to depart peacefully, and be given time in which to quit the land.

There are many other Acts of Parliament and Common Law rights, and the fisheries manager is advised *always* to seek legal clarification.

Appendix 6

Genetic developments and salmonid fishery management

In stillwater fisheries there is a demand for interspecific fish crosses as a novelty. In practical terms, production of large numbers is not feasible at the moment due to high cost and lack of demand. However, the following crosses have been produced, and may be of interest to fish farmers.

Female rainbow × male brown	= 'brownbow'
Female brownbow × male brown	= 'sunbeam' (F_1 backcross)
Brook char × brown	= 'zebra' or 'tiger' (low fertility)
Brook char × lake char	= 'splake' (fertile)
Brook char × rainbow	= 'cheetah' (low fertility)
Brook char × Atlantic salmon	(no popular name)

Of much greater use is the elimination of early sexual maturity in male rainbow trout which gives rise to the 'black rainbow': these fish are noted for their poor condition, unpleasant appearance and taste, and relatively poor growth rate. Elimination of sexual characteristics can be achieved in several ways, including: production of sterile fish; production of all female fish; radical delay in maturity, and selective killing of male eggs.

Sterile fish can be produced by surgical castration or by administration of a high concentration of sex steroids. Other techniques are being developed, involving thermal shock to the eggs and irradiation of fish sperm. All-female fish can be produced successfully in salmonids by two methods involving the use of hormones in the feed.

Appendix 7

Conversion factors and useful equivalents

Weight

28.4g	= 1oz
1kg (1 000g)	= 2.2lb (35.27oz)
1 tonne	= 2 205lb

Volume

4.55 litre	= 1 gallon
1 litre (1 000cc or 1 000ml)	= 0.22 gallons
1 litre	= 1.76 pints (0.26 US gallons)
28.3 litres	= 1ft^3
1 foot^3	= 6.22 gallons
0.764m^3	= 1 yard^3
1 metre^3	= 1.308 yard^3
1m^3	= 35.31ft^3

Length

25.4mm (2.54cm)	= 1 inch
30.48cm	= 1 foot
0.914m	= 1 yard
1 metre	= 39.37 inches

Area

0.836m^2	= 1 yard^2
1m^2	= 1.196 yard^2
4 840 yard^2	= 1 acre
2.47 acres	= 1 hectare

Water Equivalent

10lb (4.54kg)	= 1 gallon
6.23 gall (28.3kg)	= 1ft^3

Flow rate

1.26ml per second	= 1 gallon per hour
1 litre per second	= 13.2 gallons per minute
28.3 litre per sec (373.8gpm)	= 1ft^3 per second
538 272 gall per day	= 1ft^3 per second

4.546 megalitres = 1 million gallons
1m³ = 80.6 gallons

Temperature

on the centigrade scale 0°C and 100°C represent the freezing and boiling points respectively of water (at standard pressure). To convert Fahrenheit (°F) degrees to Centigrade (°C) use the formula:

$$°F = (°C \times 9/5) + 32$$

Appendix 8

Common animal and plant names, with scientific equivalents

Birds

Black-headed gull	– *Larus ridibundus* (L)
Cormorant	– *Phalacrocorax carbo* (L)
Great black-backed gull	– *Larus marinus* (L)
Great crested grebe	– *Podiceps cristatus* (L)
Grey heron	– *Ardea cinerea* (L)
Herring gull	– *Larus argentatus* (L)
Kingfisher	– *Alcedo atthis* (L)
Lesser black-backed gull	– *Larus fuscus* (L)
Little grebe (dabchick)	– *Podiceps ruficollis* (L)
Tufted duck	– *Aythya fuligula* (L)

Mammals

Coypu	– *Myocaster coypus* (Molina)
Mink	– *Mustela vison* (L)
Mole	– *Talpa europaea* (L)
Otter	– *Lutra lutra* (L)
Rat, common	– *Rattus norvegicus* (Berkenhart)
Water vole	– *Arvicola terrestris* (L)

Fish

Barbel	– *Barbus barbus* (L)
Bitterling	– *Rhodeus sericeus* (Bloch)
Bleak	– *Alburnus alburnus* (L)
Bream	– *Abramis brama* (L)
Bullhead	– *Cottus gobio* (L)
Carp	– *Cyprinus carpio* (L)
Carp, chinese grass	– *Ctenopharyngoden idella* (Val)
Carp, crucian	– *Carassius carassius* (L)
Char	– *Salvelinus alpinus* (L)
Chub	– *Leuciscus cephalus* (L)
Dab	– *Limanda limanda* (L)
Dace	– *Leuciscus leuciscus* (L)
Eel	– *Anguilla anguilla* (L)

Flounder	– *Platichthys flesus* (L)
Goldfish	– *Carassius auratus* (L)
Grayling	– *Thymallus thymallus* (L)
Gudgeon	– *Gobio gobio* (L)
Lamprey, brook	– *Lampetra planeri* (Bloch)
Lamprey, river	– *Lampetra fluviatilis* (L)
Loach stone	– *Noemacheilus barbatulus* (L)
Minnow	– *Phoxinus phoxinus* (L)
Mullet, thick-lipped	– *Crenimugil labrosus* (Risso)
Mullet, thin-lipped	– *Chelon ramada* (Risso)
Perch	– *Perca fluviatilis* (L)
Pike	– *Esox lucius* (L)
Roach	– *Rutilus rutilus* (L)
Rudd	– *Scardinius erythrophthalmus* (L)
Ruffe	– *Gymnocephalus cernua* (L)
Salmon	– *Salmo salar* (L)
Stickleback, 3 spined	– *Gasterosteus aculeatus* (L)
Tench	– *Tinca tinca* (L)
Trout, American brook	– *Salvelinus fontinalis* (Mitchill)
Trout, brown	– *Salmo trutta fario* (L)
Trout, rainbow	– *Salmo gairdneri* (Richardson)
Trout sea	– *Salmo trutta trutta* (L)
Zander	– *Stizostedion lucioperca* (L)

Invertebrates

Beetle larvae	– *Coleptera*
Caddis larvae	– *Trichoptera*
Freshwater hog louse	– *Ascellus aquaticus*
Freshwater shrimp	– *Gammarus* spp
Pea mussels	– *Pisidium* spp
Swan mussels	– *Anodonta* spp

Parasites

Eye fluke	– *Diplostomum spathaceum* (L)
Fish louse	– *Argulus* spp
Leech	– *Piscicola* spp
Tapeworm-pike	– *Triaenophorus nodulosus* (Pallus)
Tapeworm	– *Diphylobothrium* spp
Tapeworm	– *Ligula* spp
Whirling disease	– *Myxosoma cerebralis* (Hofer)

Plants

Amphibious bistort	– *Polygonum amphibium* (L)
Arrowhead	– *Sagittaria sagittifolia* (L)
Bullrush	– *Scirpus lacustris* (L)
Bur-reed	– *Sparganium erectum* (L)
Canadian pond weed	– *Elodea canadensis* (Michx)

Common reed	– *Phragmites communis* (Trin)
Duckweed	– *Lemna minor* (L)
Frogbit	– *Hydrocharis morsus-ranae* (L)
Great water dock	– *Rumex hydrolapathum* (Huds)
Hornwort	– *Ceratophyllum demersum* (L)
Ivy-leaved duckweed	– *Lemna trisulca* (L)
Mare's tail	– *Hippuris vulgaris* (L)
Pondweed	– *Potomogeton* spp
Reed grass	– *Glyceria maxima* (Hartm)
Reed mace	– *Typha latifolia* (L)
Stonewort	– *Chara* spp
Watercress	– *Nasturtium officinale* (R. Br)
Water crowfoot	– *Ranunculus aquatilis* (L)
Water lilies	– *Nymphaea alba* (L)
	– *Nuphar lutea* (L)
Water milfoil	– *Myriophyllum* spp
Water plantain	– *Alisma plantago aquatica* (L)
Water starwort	– *Callitriche stagnalis* (Scop)

Trees

Alder	– *Alnus glutinosa* (L)
Ash	– *Fraxinus excelsior* (L)
Crack willow	– *Salix fragilis* (L)
Hairy birch	– *Betula pubescens* (Ehrh)
Oak	– *Quercus robur* (L)
White willow	– *Salix alba* (L)

Reading list

Part 1: The resource   BAGENAL T B (1973) *Identification of British Fishes*. Educational Publishers.

BAGENAL T B (1978) *Methods for assessment of fish production in freshwaters*. IBP Handbook No. 3. Blackwell Scientific Publc.

COOPER M J (1979) Large river monitoring. *Proc. of IFM Annual Study Course*.

ENGLEHARDT W (1973) *Pond Life*. Burke Publishing.

HARRIS J R (1973) *An angler's entomology*. New Naturalist Collins.

HARTLEY G W (1980) Electrical fishing apparatus and its safety. *Fisheries Management* **6** (3): 73–77.

HOFFERMAN G and MEYER F P (1974) *Parasites of Freshwater Fishes*. T F H Publishers.

HYNES H B N (1971) *The biology of polluted waters*. Liverpool University Press.

HYNES H B N (1972) *Ecology of running waters*. Liverpool University Press.

JONES J R E (1964) *Fish and River Pollution*. Butterworth.

JONES R (1979) *Materials and methods used in marking experiments in fishery research*. FAO Fisheries Technical Rep. No. 190.

KENNEDY G J A, STRANGE C D (1981) Efficiency of electric fishing for salmonids in relation to river width. *Fisheries Management* **12** (2): 55–60.

MACAN T T (1970) *A guide to freshwater animals*. Longman.

MACAN T T, WORTHINGTON E D (1972) *Life in lakes and rivers*. New Naturalist, Fontana.

MACAN T T (1974) *Freshwater Ecology*. Longmans.

MAITLAND P S (1972) *Key to British Freshwater Fishes*. Freshwater Biological Association, Science Publication No 27.

MILLS D H (1971) *An introduction to freshwater ecology*. Oliver and Boyd.

MOSS B (1980) *Ecology of freshwaters*. Blackwell Scientific Public.

MUSS B J, DAHLSTROM P (1971) *Collins guide to Freshwater Fishes of Britain and Europe*. Collins.

ODUM E P (1959) *Fundamentals of Ecology*. W. B. Saunders Co.

PICKERING A D (1982) *Stress and fish*. Academic Press.

PITCHER T J, HART J B (1982) *Fisheries Ecology*. Croom Helm.

PRATT M M (1975) *Better angling with simple science*. Fishing News Books.

SEYMOUR R (1970) *Fishery management and keepering*. Charles Knight and Co. Ltd.

VARLEY M E (1967) *British Freshwater Fishes*. Fishing News Books.

VIBERT R (1976) *Fishing with Electricity*. Fishing News Books.

IFM Certificate and Diploma booklet(s) on *Freshwater Biology*.

IFM Diploma booklet on *Fish Diseases*.

IFM Certificate and Diploma booklets on *Water Quality*.

Part 2: Management

THE ANGLING FOUNDATION (1974) *The creation of low cost fisheries*. 7 Swallow Road, London W1R 7HD.

BEHRENDT A (1977) *The management of angling waters*. Andre Deutsch.

BIRCH E (1964) *The management of coarse fishing waters*. J. Baker, London.

BURSCHE E M (1971) *A Handbook of Water Plants*. F. Warne.

CUTHBERT J H (1979) Food studies of feral mink. *Fisheries Management* **10** (1): 17–26.

FROST W E, BROWN M E (1967) *The Trout*. Collins.

GREGORY M (1974) *Angling and the Law* (Second Edition). Charles Knight, London.

HASLAM S, SINKER C, WOLSELY P (1975) *British water plants*. Field Studies Council, Preston Montford, Shrewsbury.

HOPKINS T, BRASSLEY P (1982) *Wildlife of rivers and canals*. Moorland Publishing, Station Street, Ashbourne.

JONES J W (1959) *The Salmon*. Collins.

KEBLE MARTIN W (1969) *The concise British Flora in Colour*. Elbury Press, M. Joseph.

MAFF Booklet *Code of practice for the use of herbicides on weeds in watercourses and lakes*. Free from MAFF Pesticides Branch, Ruskin Avenue, Kent TW9 4DN.

MARTON R K (1971) *Man and Bird*. The New Naturalist. Collins, London.

MILLS D (1979) *Bird predation – current views*. IFM Annual Study Course Proc.

RSPCA (1981) *Book of Mammals*. Collins, London.

STWA *The use of herbicides in water supply catchments*. STWA, Abelson House, Coventry Road, Birmingham.

SEYMOUR R (1970) *Fishery management and river keepering*. Charles Knight.

SEYMOUR R, GREGORY M (1970) *All for Fishing*. Charles Knight.

STOTT B (1977) On the question of the introduction of the grass carp into the UK. *Fisheries Management* **8** (3): 63–71.

TILLER T (1977) *Practical vermin control*. 9th Two Lakes Training Course Report 75–81. Janssen Services.

WHEELER A (1978) *Key to the fishes of Northern Europe*. F. Warne.

WISDOM A S (1979) *The law of rivers and watercourses*. Shaw and Sons.

WSAC (1980) *Conservation and land drainage guidelines*.

IFM booklets on the law.

IFM Certificate and Diploma booklets on *Fisheries Management*.

Part 3: Exploitation

BARDACH J, RYTHER J, CLARNEY W M (1977) *Aquaculture*. Wiley Interscience, 2nd Ed.

BRYANT P, JAUNCEY K, ATTACK T (1980) *Backyard fish farming*. Prism Press.

BURGESS J, *Trammel netting*. Bridport-Gundry Ltd, Dorset.

BURGESS J, *Drift, Gill and Ray netting*. Bridport-Gundry Ltd, Dorset.

DAVIES H S (1961) *Culture and Diseases of Game Fishes*. University of California Press and Cambridge University Press, London.

DRUMMOND-SEDGWICK S (1976) *Trout Farming Handbook*. Seeley, Service, London. Revised edition.

FORREST D M (1976) *Eel Capture, Culture, Processing and Marketing*. Fishing News Books.

GARNER J (1962) *How to make and set nets*. Fishing News Books.

GREENBERG D G (1980) *Trout Farming*. Chilton Co., Philadelphia.

HICKLING C F (1971) *Fish Culture*. Faber and Faber, London (2nd Edition).

HUET M (1972) *Textbook of Fish Culture*. Fishing News Books.

KARLSSOM S (1977) The freshwater crayfish. *Fish Farmer Magazine*.

LEITRITZ E and LEWIS C (1980) *Trout and Salmon Culture* (Hatchery Methods). Fish Bulletin No. 164 of the State of California Department of Fish and Game. Publication 4100 Agricultural Science Publications, University of California.

Lowestoft Laboratory Leaflet No. 35. *Fish Cultivation Research*. MAFF Fisheries Laboratory, Pakefield Road, Lowestoft, Suffolk.

MILLS D (1971) *Salmon and Trout: A resource, its ecology, conservation and management*. Oliver and Boyd, Edinburgh.

NETBOY A (1968) *The Atlantic Salmon. A vanishing species?* Faber and Faber, London.

REAY P (1979) *Aquaculture*. Institute of Biology Publication 106.

ROBERTS R J, SHEPHERD C J (1975) *Handbook of Trout and Salmon Diseases*. Fishing News Books.

ROBERTS R J (1978) *Fish Pathology*. Bailliere Tindall.

Scottish District Salmon Fishery Boards, Association of, (1977) *Salmon Fisheries of Scotland*. Fishing News Books.

SINHA V R P, JONES J W (1975) *The European Freshwater Eel*. Liverpool University Press.

STEVENSON J P (1980) *Trout Farming Manual*. Fishing News Books.

TESCH F W (1977) *The Eel Biology and Management of Anguillid Eels.*
   Chapman and Hall, London.
USUI A (1974) *Eel Culture*. Fishing News Books.
IFM Certificate booklet on *Fishing Methods*.
IFM Certificate and Diploma booklets on fish propagation.

Subject index

Other books published by Fishing News Books Ltd

Free catalogue available on request

Advances in aquaculture
Advances in fish science and
  technology
Aquaculture practices in Taiwan
Atlantic salmon: its future
Better angling with simple science
British freshwater fishes
Commercial fishing methods
Control of fish quality
Culture of bivalve molluscs
Echo sounding and sonar for fishing
The edible crab and its fishery in
  British waters
Eel capture, culture, processing and
  marketing
Eel culture
Engineering, economics and fisheries
  management
European inland water fish: a
  multilingual catalogue
FAO catalogue of fishing gear designs
FAO catalogue of small scale fishing
  gear
FAO investigates ferro-cement fishing
  craft
Farming the edge of the sea
Fibre ropes for fishing gear
Fish and shellfish farming in coastal
  waters
Fish catching methods of the world
Fisheries of Australia
Fisheries oceanography and ecology
Fisheries sonar
Fishermen's handbook
Fishery products
Fishing boats and their equipment
Fishing boats of the world 1
Fishing boats of the world 2
Fishing boats of the world 3
The fishing cadet's handbook
Fishing ports and markets
Fishing with electricity
Fishing with light
Freezing and irradiation of fish
Glossary of UK fishing gear terms
Handbook of trout and salmon diseases

Handy medical guide for seafarers
How to make and set nets
Introduction to fishery by-products
The lemon sole
A living from lobsters
Making and managing a trout lake
Marine fisheries ecosystem
Marine pollution and sea life
Marketing in fisheries and aquaculture
Mending of fishing nets
Modern deep sea trawling gear
Modern fishing gear of the world 1
Modern fishing gear of the world 2
Modern fishing gear of the world 3
More Scottish fishing craft and their
  work
Multilingual dictionary of fish and fish
  products
Navigation primer for fishermen
Netting materials for fishing gear
Pair trawling and pair seining
Pelagic and semi-pelagic trawling gear
Penaeid shrimps – their biology and
  management
Planning of aquaculture development
Power transmission and automation
  for ships and submersibles
Refrigeration on fishing vessels
Salmon and trout farming in Norway
Salmon fisheries of Scotland
Scallop and queen fisheries in the
  British Isles
Scallops and the diver fisherman
Seafood fishing for amateur and
  professional
Seine fishing
Squid jigging from small boats
Stability and trim of fishing vessels
The stern trawler
Study of the sea
Textbook of fish culture
Training fishermen at sea
Trends in fish utilization
Trout farming manual
Tuna distribution and migration
Tuna fishing with pole and line